LIVERPOOL

The Golden Years

The publishers would like to thank the following companies for their support in the production of this book

Brookes Bell Group

EG Everton Glass

Frank Rogers Building Contractor Ltd

GETRAG FORD Transmissions

John Mason International

Merchant Taylors' School

Nugent Care

Rathbone Brothers Plc

Tilney Bestinvest

The Venmore Group

First published in Great Britain by True North Books Limited
England HX3 6SN
01422 244555
www.truenorthbooks.com

LIVERPOOL

The Golden Years

CONTENTS

INTRODUCTION

For all of us, memories are the currency which we use to record the changes and progress in our everyday lives and to fix our place as individuals in the greater scheme of things. This is the latest publication in our 'Memories' series of publications, covering nostalgic reflections of towns and cities throughout the UK. In this new book we will be meandering through a pictorial cross-section of life in Liverpool over the last 100 years or so, to help satisfy the longing we all get from time to time, to recall memories of a different era that now seems better or simpler.

As we get older it is often easier to take a step back, and to view events and developments with a clearer sense of prospective. Our aim has been to assist in this respect by presenting a publication relevant to the area capable of rekindling memories of days gone by in an entertaining and informative manner. Looking through the pages of this book it is interesting to reflect on exactly how much change has taken place in the area over a short period, relative to its long history. Many of these photographs are unique and will inevitably remind us of experiences and events in our lives, of our families and of those whose influence and support has touched us to a greater or lesser degree.

Defining features about nostalgia are universal and can bring back fond memories from a time gone by. Recent research shows that nostalgia can counteract loneliness, boredom and anxiety. Couples feel closer and look happier when they're sharing nostalgic memories. People generally get a 'Warm Glow' inside when relating to events and occasions in the past and enjoy reminiscences about how things used to be – even when these events sometimes have a painful side. When people speak wistfully of the past, they typically become more optimistic and inspired about the future.

We can all remember events surrounding friends and family, holidays, weddings, special occasions and nights out in Liverpool. So let your mind wander and think of the youthful days at the dance hall or courting in one of the many cinemas in the city. Be entertained as we take you on a sentimental journey through the pages of Liverpool - The Golden Years.... Happy Memories!

TEXT — BRENDAN O' NEILL, ANDREW MITCHELL, STEVE AINSWORTH
PHOTOGRAPH RESEARCH — BRENDAN O' NEILL
DESIGNER — SEAMUS MOLLOY
BUSINESS DEVELOPMENT MANAGER — PETER PREST

IN VICTORIAN & EDWARDIAN DAYS

Church Street took its name from St Peter's Church, built in the first decade of the 18th century, and demolished in 1923. The horse-drawn tram in the picture from the late 19th century was on its way to the Pierhead. The open staircase to the top deck was typical of the early tramcar design that would be repeated even when electrification of the line was introduced.

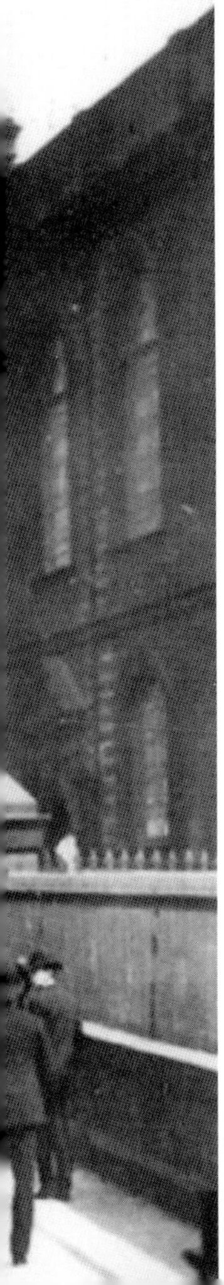

Bevington Bush is a small outpost in the city of Liverpool. It lies in a little kink between Scotland Road and Leeds Street. Some 250 years ago, it was a pastoral area with shrubbery around, hence its name. It was formerly a pleasant spot where city dwellers could take a Sunday stroll. However, in mid-Victorian times it became the site of one of England's first council house developments. Here, in 1900, a number of young residents gathered around Seth Davy, a street entertainer thought by some to hail originally from West Africa, but more likely to have his roots in Jamaica. He sang ditties and showed off dancing dolls that had obviously taken the fancy of these youngsters. The dolls were attached to a plank and vibrated or 'danced' when the spar was struck. Seth died in 1902 and is immortalised in the folk song 'Whisky on a Sunday', recorded by such artists as the Dubliners and Max Boyce. A version by Danny Doyle topped the Irish charts in 1967.

Above: Central Station opened on 2 March, 1874, replacing Brunswick as the Cheshire Lines Committee terminus. The three-storey station fronted Ranelagh Street. Although a busy one, the main station was closed under the Beeching purge on the railways in the 1960s and most of its services were diverted to Lime Street. The High Level station was demolished in 1973, having served some time as a car park. The underground section dates from 1892 and continues to operate successfully today.

Below: Lord Street, just before the Great War, was a thriving retail area with many grand buildings that were a joy to behold. It is still the main part of the city where people love to do their shopping, but its face was altered dramatically during the early 1940s. Much of the locality was obliterated by Luftwaffe bombing raids that destroyed so much of our architectural heritage. When rebuilding work was undertaken in peacetime, the original ornate, attractive structures were replaced by less interesting ones that relied heavily upon the rectangle for their inspiration. New buildings were erected as rubble was cleared from the waste land that was the legacy of the Blitz, but such had been the devastation that it seemed an eternity before all the scars were removed.

Left: The view across the Haymarket shows William Brown Street, with the Wellington Monument beyond the Museum and Central Library. The column rises above neighbouring buildings at the junction with Lime Street. After the death of Arthur Wellesley, to give the Duke of Wellington his birth name, a competition was established to appoint an architect to design a suitable memorial to honour the former Prime Minister and leader of troops at the Battle of Waterloo. The ideas of the Lawson brothers, from Edinburgh, were adopted and work on the column and figure began. A variety of delays led to the work not being completed until 1865, 13 years after Wellington's demise. The overall height is 132 feet and there are 169 steps within the column that lead up to a viewing platform.

Below: This was how Lime Street appeared in Edwardian times. That first decade of the last century saw great changes in modes of transport on our streets. Motor cars started to appear, electrified routes for trams were established and horse-drawn vehicles began to say their goodbyes. In recent times, statues of Ken Dodd and Bessie Braddock adorn the railway concourse, but a century ago it was those erected over the way outside St George's Hall in honour of such national figures as Disraeli that took the eye. Queen Victoria and her husband, Prince Albert, are also celebrated as the figures on horseback. She is shown as she looked in her younger days and the sculptor, Thomas Thornycroft, has given us something different from the sight of the ageing widow more often depicted.

Right: The main advert on the side of this Edwardian tram makes for interesting reading as Van Houten is a name that has been important in the seemingly restricted world of cocoa powder for nearly two centuries. The company was founded in Amsterdam in 1815 by Coenraad Johannes Van Houten, but it was in 1828 that Van Houten invented a process for pressing cocoa into a soluble product. Very soon his cocoa and chocolate powders conquered the hearts of thousands of chocolate lovers. At one time, this was a beverage prepared by grandmothers for a goodnight brew. Now, sachets can be found in vending machines in offices across Europe. The building behind the tram is the old Technical School, Museum and Reading Room.

Below: Breck Road in Anfield still has a number of independent retail outlets today, just as it boasted back in Edwardian times when this image was captured from a position just southwest of the junction with Esmond Street, on the right. In more recent times, a fireplace shop and hairdresser's occupied opposite corners here. This was something of a rough and ready district back then and, sadly, the area has something of a poor reputation for social problems in this day and age too. Holy Trinity Church, seen in the distance, was built in 1847 and continues to offer a source of inspiration for its parishioners. Its crypt was developed in the 2000s into a community centre with a hall, relaxation room and kitchen.

Below: This photograph shows how public transport had become more comfortable for passengers by the 1920s. The brewery advert on the leading tram was for Walkers Ales founded by Peter Walker in Scotland before he expanded the company with premises in Burton and more locally, in Warrington. The company merged with Cains in 1921 and was to become part of the Tetley empire in 1960.

Facing page: We all know about the General Strike of 1926, but many locals are also well aware from histories related to them by grandparents and even older relatives of the general transport strike in 1911. It came at a time when the authorities were anxious about the upsurge in people power, as demonstrated by the growing influence of trade unions and women's emancipation movements. Action began in mid-June when a national seaman's strike was announced. Workers in other industries, particularly the dockyards, railways and road transport, soon withdrew their labour in support over a period of turmoil that would last for over two months. After a city centre rally held in August attracted a crowd of 85,000, police mounted a number of baton charges to disperse gatherings during the day. There were 350 reported casualties and troops were deployed to assist in keeping order. Soldiers of the 18th Hussars, seen here camped on Edge Lane, were used and they opened fire on a group in Vauxhall Road, killing two of the protesters. An inquest would later record a verdict of 'justifiable homicide'. This came as no surprise to the strikers.

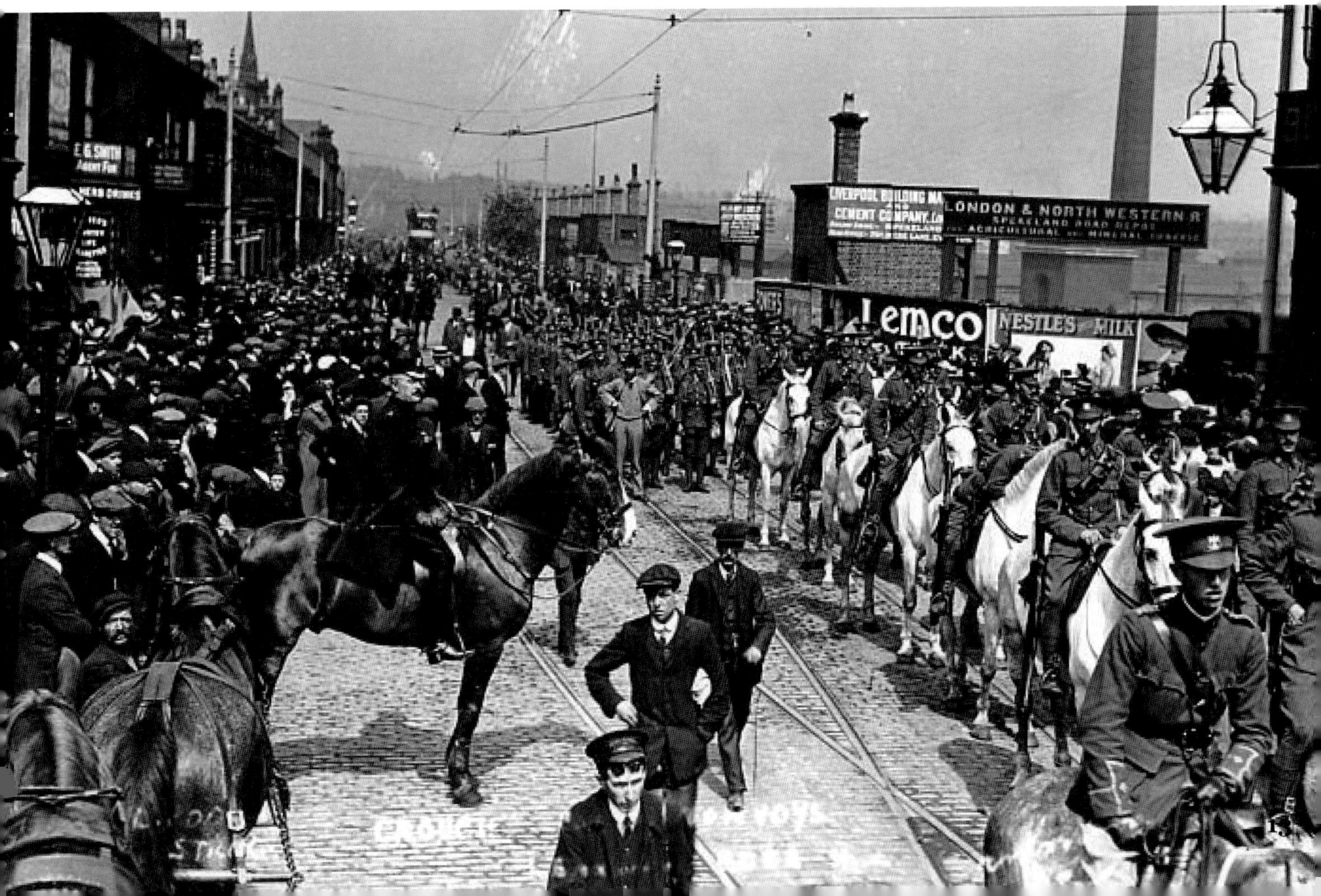
E. G. SMITH
LIVERPOOL BUILDING MA
CEMENT COMPANY, L
LONDON & NORTH WESTERN R
Lemco
NESTLE'S MILK

THROUGH THE CITY

Looking at this fabulous photograph from the late 1920s, it is hard to gauge the scale and prospective of how this image was conceived. The distance between Queen Victoria monument in Derby Square, and the Grade I listed Town Hall building, looks much shorter than it is in reality. In any event, it gives a fantastic snap-shot of the times, with trams noisily trundelling down Castle Street past the Midland Bank building and the subterranean public toilets on the left. We can also see the fashion conscious women of the day wearing the iconic cloche hat of the twenties decade, that will ever be associated with the sophistication and glamour of the era. The 'Roaring Twenties' as it became known, was a decade of great economic growth and widespread prosperity, and a decade when dance music came to dominate our lives.

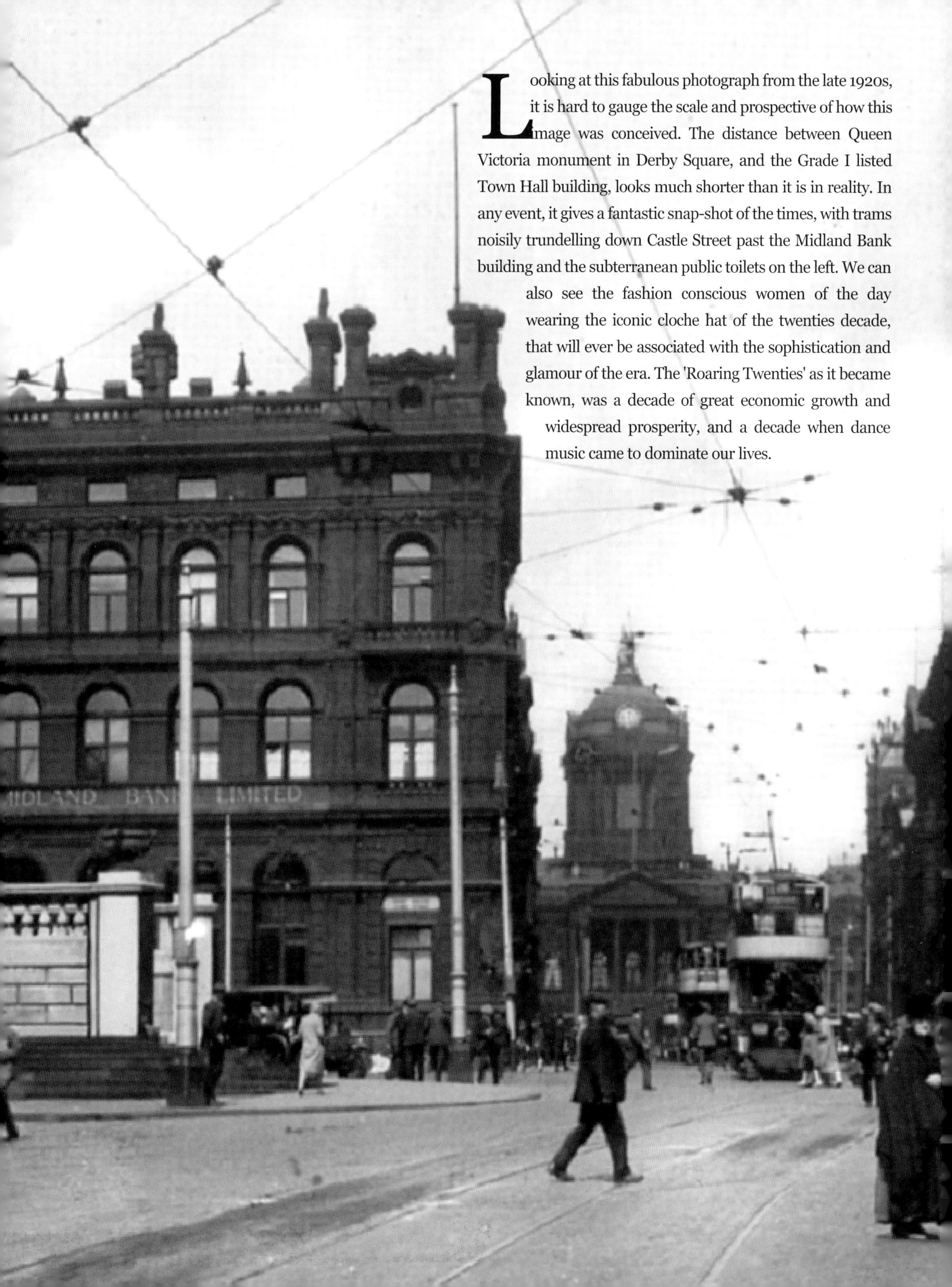

Above: With head offices on Great Nelson Street, WH Colley and Sons was a very successful wholesale fruit and vegetable supplier for most of the last century. The size of the workforce seen here demonstrates how well the business was doing nearly a century ago. You can tell the social standing of the men we can see from their headgear alone. Manual workers almost exclusively sported flat caps, while office and managerial staff largely showed off a fashion for homburgs and trilbies. No doubt the young woman in the frame will have been one of the up and coming breed of females who were developing a head for business. New roads and flyovers abound in this area now but, coincidentally, Great Nelson Street is still home to a large wholesale business as Bestway has a large cash and carry outlet there.

Below: A 1932 shot taken in Derby Square. The memorial to Queen Victoria somehow managed to survive the wartime air raids of the early 1940s, but most of the buildings in her vicinity were badly damaged or destroyed by the hail of high explosives that rained down upon us in those dark days. The monument was erected on the site of a castle that dated from around the 1230s. The fortress was commissioned by William de Ferrers, 4th Earl of Derby. The foundation stone for the structure in honour of Victoria was laid in 1902, the year after her death. It was not until 1906 that it was officially unveiled. By then, we were halfway through the reign of her successor.

Left: Viewed from a position just below where Davies Street joins Dale Street, the main building in view is that of the city's Municipal Offices. These were built in the 1860s to house the rapidly expanding number of council employees, particularly administrative staff. Created to a design by John Weightman, the Corporation Surveyor, they were completed by his successor ER Robson in 1868, and are still in public use today. There is a distinct Renaissance feel to the architectural nature that has obvious French and Italian influences. At its centre, there is a tower with a strange, steeply pitched stone roof, based on C.H. Barry's Halifax Town Hall. The handsome sandstone figures around the balcony represent the industries, arts and sciences of the city.

Every city needs a quiet oasis from the hustle, bustle and hurly-burly of everyday life. These folk have found a comfortable spot to chat, stroll or simply lose themselves in a good book before returning to the office or setting off back home. The Coronation Gardens, taking their name from the day in 1953 when many of us saw a television programme for the first time as Queen Elizabeth II made her way into Westminster Abbey.

Unfortunately, the life of these gardens was surprisingly short, hardly lasting a couple of decades. They were but a temporary measure created on top of one of the many ugly bomb sites that still blighted the landscape, and would disappear when the area was redeveloped. Looking over the heads of the readers we can see Paradise Street on the right, heading towards Whitechapel. Bunney's department store is on the corner.

Left: The Adelphi Hotel, on Ranelagh Place, is the third such establishment to have graced this site. The first was built for hotelier, James Radley, in 1826 where Ranelagh Gardens had once been. They were part of the first open public space to be found in Liverpool and during the 18th century gave people a chance to socialise in the open air and to enjoy the sight of the flower beds and promenade along the walkways. Radley's hotel was replaced by another in 1876, which was taken over by the Midland Railway Company in 1892. The present building was built in the years just before World War One. Designed by Frank Atkinson, it was referred to as 'the most luxurious hotel outside London'. A regular, well-heeled clientele favoured it as they waited to take a berth on one of the ocean going liners that frequented the port.

Top right: This is a view of Queensway and William Brown Street as recognised by those of us who can recall the immediate post-war era that saw the birth of today's pensioners from the 'baby-boomer' years. The toll booths on the left are access points through which entry to the Birkenhead Tunnel could be gained. The Queensway route under the river was built in the interwar years as a result of the rise in the use of private cars and lorries. During the 1920s, it was a common sight to observe long queues of traffic waiting to use the Mersey Ferry terminal. The project took nine years to complete and when the tunnel was opened on 18 July, 1934, by King George V it was, at the time, the world's longest underwater tunnel. It held that record for a further 24 years.

Right: Today, Bold Street is regarded by its retail clientele as being part of the more prestigious aspect of city centre shopping. It boasts a significant number of independent businesses, both large and small, and includes several smart cafés and watering holes. The car that we see in this late 1950s scene would not have much access to Bold Street now as most of it is pedestrianised. In much earlier times, this was the centre of a rope making industry. Rope was measured by being laid out from one end of the street to the other as this was the appropriate length required by sailing ships. The street was named after Jonas Bold, a slave trader who became Mayor in 1802.

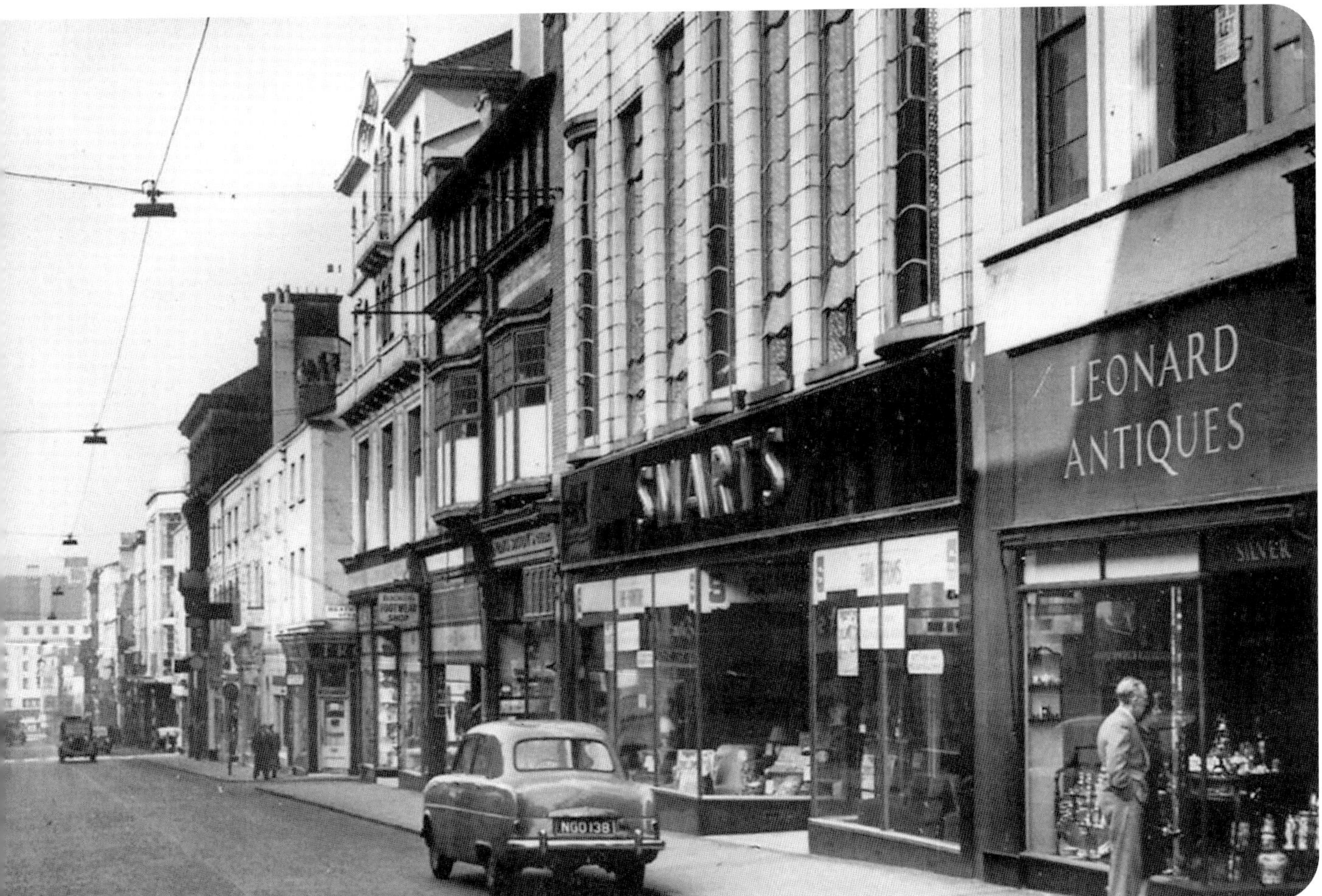
SMARTS
LEONARD
ANTIQUES
SILVER
NGO 138

Saxone's, on Church Street, in the mid-1950s was where a girl might have bought her first pair of stiletto shoes. They were great for the look, but a nightmare in which to walk as she toddled along the pavement, desperate not to get a heel caught in one of the cracks. If she did, there was a loud 'click' and she came down to earth

with a bump. Barker & Dobson, opposite Saxone, is the confectionery manufacturer perhaps best known for its Everton mints. These black and white humbugs are a reminder of the colours worn for a while in the early days of Everton Football Club.

SURROUNDING AREAS

The trams in a companion photograph trundled along the newly electrified line, not long after the start of the 20th century. The woman who had just alighted from the No 7 car was dressed quite formally. In those days, a true lady would not be seen out and about in casual clothing. In this scene there is a nice contrast between the old and new. On one side, we have up to date transport and, on the other, a hand propelled barrow next to a horse-drawn cart.

Above: The sands at Waterloo, just by Crosby, are easily accessible for Merseysiders. They are close to the area along the coast selected in the early 2000s by artist Antony Gormley as the spot where he would erect a series of lifelike statues. Called 'Another Place', his creation stretches out from the shore and into the sea. The only figures you could see in the accompanying photograph were real enough, though. Children played happily in the sand, building castles adorned with little flags, or they wandered out into pools armed with small fishing nets. Such simple pleasures meant that they were entertained for hours whilst mum and dad took it easy on their deckchairs. Even so, the adults kept an eye out for their youngsters as the waters and mudflats made parts of this section of the coastline dangerous for the unwary.

Below: In this view of South Road, a small group of shoppers has assembled outside William Timpson's shoe shop on the corner with Neville Road. This chain store was established on Oldham Road, Manchester, in 1870. A clothes shop could be found on the Waterloo site in modern times.

Below and right: The children we can see had been wandering along Beech Lane and Menlove Avenue, just above The Vineries and close to Allerton Park Golf Club, without realising that they were not far from a place that would, in time, attract visitors from all over the world. John Lennon, one of the Beatles fab four, spent most of his childhood at Mendips, 251 Menlove Avenue. This was where his Aunt Mimi and Uncle George lived. They were a childless couple who were happy to offer a stable home to the six year old John, a boy who had suffered emotionally being brought up in a broken home. Not far away from this tree lined boulevard was a place called Strawberry Field, a Salvation Army children's home. A fête was held here each summer and visiting it was one of the treats that the young John enjoyed. The name was to provide an inspiration for the title of his compositions. Another of the group's well-known songs was named for the address of the tram terminus that is depicted in the accompanying image. This is Penny Lane where the No 46 and No 99 routes began, leading to Walton, Old Swan and the city centre. The terminus had a purpose-built shelter, with a passenger waiting room and public toilets. The 'Strawberry Fields Forever' and 'Penny Lane' double A side single was released in early 1967. Having had a run of 11 consecutive No 1 hits with their official singles' releases, it was a surprise to many when it ended with the record peaking at Number 2 in the hit parade.

Above: This is how we remember the village of Woolton in the late 1950s. It is one of the more affluent of Liverpool's suburbs. Apart from some changes to the street furniture and narrowing of the entry to Allerton Road from Woolton Street, this is how the village looks well over half a century later as well. Today, the buildings on view consist of a branch of HSBC, an Indian restaurant and a health food shop. The little white building to the right is Salisbury Lodge, a beauty salon.

The tram advertising Crawford's Cream Crackers headed away from the racecourse, on Ormskirk Road, and travelled along Warbreck Moor Road. Behind it lay the Sefton Arms, a pub that was renamed in the late 20th century as the Red Rum Grill, after the three time Grand National winner. Even more recently, the site has been home to an Indian restaurant. The action photograph, taken during an event at the Aintree Racecourse, shows one of its iconic fences. This was near where Devon Loch came to grief in 1956. Ridden by future thriller writer, Dick Francis, the horse was comfortably leading the race when, just yards from the winning post, it inexplicably leapt into the air and collapsed onto its stomach. Many thought that a shadow from the adjacent water jump fooled the horse into jumping, but the truth will never be known. ESB, ridden by David Dick, was the winner and Devon Loch did not even finish.

Crosby residents must have invested heavily in Morris Minors for their family motoring, if the 1958 view along Coronation Road is any evidence. The model name was first used by Morris Motors in 1928 for a small four seater saloon that stayed in production for six years. The name was resurrected after the last war for a new version, the one we came to know and love so well as an icon of this country's motor industry. Crosby is a town in Sefton with Viking roots, its name meaning 'village with the cross' in old Norse. Cherie Blair, the former Prime Minister's wife, TV presenter Anne Robinson and the late Kenny Everett, the comedian and DJ, were all brought up here. They would have played on the beach that runs close to their childhood homes, but not in the 1920s when this camp scene took place. It looks like a refugee village in the Middle East, but this was Merseysiders having fun in the decade after the First World War.

Sefton Park attracted children and the young at heart to sail their model yachts on the boating lake. It is a peaceful idyll of some 200 acres that is, perhaps, the best loved of all of Liverpool's open spaces as it has a delightful natural feel. It was once part of Toxteth's Royal Deer Park, before coming under the control of the Earl of Sefton. Designed by French landscape artist, Edouard André, and the local architect, Lewis Hornblower, the park was opened by Prince Arthur in 1872. The Punch Bowl, on Lunt Road, dates back some 200 years. Its grounds are on the site of the original Grand National racecourse. It was here that a mysterious gentleman's club, known as the Mock Corporation of Sefton, would hold its meetings.

New Brighton Tower was the tallest in the country when it was built in 1900. Sadly, a lack of maintenance during the First World War, as attention turned to more important matters, led to the structure becoming unstable. It closed in 1919 and was demolished two years later. However, the ballroom at its base continued to bring in the crowds until it was badly damaged in a fire in 1969. The lighthouse stands next to Fort Perch Rock, a historically important site in the defences of the port of Liverpool. A light had been maintained on the rock since 1683, but it was in 1827 that building of the present structure began. It stayed in use until 1973.

Right: These brave folk are making their way to Fort Perch Rock, across the causeway which separates the open sea from the relatively calm Marine Lake, in 1959. They will be dodging the waves crashing against the sea wall and hopefully making it across, as dry as they could, but their overcoats in 1959 would not be the lightweight, highly waterproof ones we know today. The heavy gabardine, woolly gloves and fabric hats would very quickly soak up any sea water that landed on these hardy souls.

Below: The New Brighton Pier was as grand as any other around the shores of Great Britain at the time of its opening in 1867. Standing next to the Ferry Pier, it was over 500 feet long and 70 feet wide. With its Pavilion Theatre, it attracted the crowds with varied concerts and shows until the theatre closed in 1923. The pier, however, continued to attract day trippers and holiday makers alike, but its years were numbered when the New Brighton Ferry ceased operations in 1971 and visitors to the pier diminished rapidly. It was soon decided, after much discussion, that the pier should be dismantled and in 1978 this fine structure and such an iconic part of New Brighton's history was sadly demolished.

A sailing school business now uses the Marine Lake at New Brighton, but when we were young it was a much more free and easy place to come. Admittedly, there were organised regattas and races, but it was generally somewhere just to hire a rowboat or small motor launch. Then you pottered off until your time was up and your number called out. The West Cheshire Sailing Club, founded in 1892, also used the lake as an alternative to the River Mersey. Growing up in New Brighton was grand as kiddies had so much entertainment right on their doorsteps.

The entrance to New Brighton Pier from Victoria Road, as seen in the above photograph from 1959, shows what a popular spot this was for holidaymakers. Known as 'Liverpool's own Blackpool', the resort's entertainments, beaches and attractions brought in hordes of visitors every summer. Even something as mundane as sailing a little boat on the children's pool provided moments of fun that were enjoyed right down the ages. The town grew in importance as a tourist centre during the Victorian age when rail connections meant that trippers and holidaymakers could access the place from right across the northwest and beyond. The pier opened in the 1860s and remained as one of New Brighton's main features until the 1970s when it was demolished. By then, the ferry across the Mersey had been abandoned and the landing stage and its pier dismantled.

EVENTS & OCCASIONS

Church Street was garlanded with decorations, bunting and streamers in readiness for the Coronation of Edward VII on 9 August, 1902. The ceremony had been delayed from June as the King had been laid low with appendicitis, once an ailment that carried a high risk of mortality. However, medical developments in anaesthesia and antisepsis meant that surgery was not quite as risky as it once had been. The monarch recovered well and the nation rejoiced in an event that had not been seen on our shores since 1838.

Bootle is a town within Sefton, traditionally linked with the docks and their associated industries. The coming of the railway in the 1840s and development of the yards along the river front in the latter half of the 19th century saw the town grow rapidly. By the time our maypole dancers and May Queen were pictured, Bootle had established its own identity in the area. We can see that the float had won second prize, or was that award given to the horse for its handsome appearance? Certainly, the 1909 Queen was the outright winner as she sat in all her splendour, surrounded by attendants and seated in the midst of dignitaries and VIPs who were turned out in all their finery.

Above: This is a flashback scene to the dark days of 1939 and Liverpool's first evacuees. Just before war was declared evacuations began on 1 September, 1939, and these children were boarding a bus to take them to safety. Children were told to bring their belongings to their departure point in a pillowcase - many came from poor families so had very little. Each child was sent with a brown paper bag containing things like corned beef, evaporated milk, biscuits, fruit and chocolate, their gas masks and a label showing their details. Like parents in all major industrial cities, those in Merseyside had to be persuaded to let their children go to strangers many miles away for an unknown length of time. Experiences varied dramatically and inevitably a lot of it was down to pure luck. Many children were terrified, others saw it as an adventure or a holiday. During World War II approximately 130,000 people were evacuated away from Merseyside. These weren't only school children, but also pregnant women, young mothers with babies and disabled adults.

Right: It was dangerous living in a big city during the war, and Liverpool was no exception. During the 'Blitz' we were the target of enemy aircraft that flew over at night and dropped many bombs. Devastation resulted and life changed for everybody, including children, but love for the Royal Family still remained strong, as we can see in this poiniant image from January 1941. For most children, the war years were a time of anxiety and for many it was a time of profound personal loss. The adults that were left had to show an unshakable resolve and a very british 'stiff upper lip' attitude to the troubles. The Union flag and a good cuppa tea reminded us of what we were fighting for.

Below left: Locals clearing up the best they can after one of a series of heavy raids which took place in December 1940, referred to as the Christmas Blitz. The Luftwaffe had again targeted Liverpool, which became the most heavily bombed area of the country, outside of London. In the aftermath, the residents of these cottages are trying to salvage what they can from the rubble. King George and his wife, Queen Elizabeth, toured many of the areas that had suffered from heavy bombing. Air raids were to continue for several months until much of the German Air Force was sent east to prepare for the invasion of Russia.

Beatlemania hit Liverpool as fans scrambled to get a glimpse of the 'Fab Four' as they arrive at the Odeon Cinema, London Road, for the northern premiere of their first feature film, 'A Hard Day's Night'. The noise reaches fever pitch as the elegant Austin Princess limousine pull up outside the cinema to drop the boys off on Friday 10 July, 1964. Earlier, John, Paul, George and Ringo had been greeted upon their arrival at Speke Airport by approximately 3,000 screaming fans. They were then whisked off in a police motorcade to a civic reception at Liverpool Town Hall, with an estimated 200,000 people – roughly a quarter of the city's population – lining the route. Following a meal, The Beatles appeared on the balcony where they waved to the gathered fans, while the Liverpool City Police Band performed Can't Buy Me Love. During a break John can be seen fooling around by trying to play a tuba taken from one of the band members. Clearly its not going well as we can see Ringo with his fingers in his ears. During the Civil Reception, each of The Beatles was presented with the keys to the city.

A Hard Day's Night was claimed as a financial and critical success and nominated for two Academy Awards: for Best Screenplay (Alun Owen), and Best Score (George Martin). By 1971 the film was estimated to have earned $11 million worldwide.

DAY'S NIGHT
12 SMASH SONG-HITS!
COIFFEUR
G GUM
BAR
THE BEATLES
12 SMASH SONG-HITS
JOHN
GEORGE
RINGO
PEDESTRIANS

Airport
Widnes (A 561)
Car Parks
Pier Head
Birkenhead (Tunnel)
Car Parks
WHSMITH
Croxley

Left: Stepping out in 'Hippie' style on Liverpool's safety first Church Street are the cast of the multi-media rock musical entitled Lonesome Stone. The groundbreaking rock opera had opened at the Rainbow Theatre in Finsbury Park, London, the previous year and was now touring throughout the UK and Europe. On a sunny Spring day in March 1974, the cast danced down Church Street, as the newly pedestrianised street was opened. We can see from the H Samuel jewellers clock it was midday and hundreds of people were lining the street to watch proceedings. It is so new, we can still see evidence of the road markings which were still to be covered. Church Street is Liverpool's main shopping area, lying between Bold Street and Lord Street and takes its name from St Peter's a church consecrated in 1704 and demolished in 1923.

Above: Seen here in this photograph from 2 May, 1984, HRH Queen Elizabeth II is seen on a walkabout much to the obvious delight of the Liverpool public. Over the years there have been numerous visits to Liverpool by the Royal couple, dating back to March 1949. The Royal party were in Liverpool for the opening of the International Garden Festival. The event was the first such event held in Britain and became the model for several others held during the 1980s and early 1990s. The aim was to revitalise tourism and the city. The festival proved to be hugely popular attracting 3,380,000 visitors to the 950,000 square metre derelict industrial site south of Herculaneum Dock, overlooking the River Mersey. A large exhibition space, the Festival Hall, formed the centrepiece of the site and housed numerous indoor exhibits.

BUILDINGS & PLACES

Below: The North Western Hotel, as its name suggests, was built by the London and North Western Railway Company on the east side of Lime Street. It was designed by Alfred Waterhouse (1830-1905), an architect best known for Victorian Gothic Revivalism, though he never restricted himself to one particular style. The son of wealthy mill owning Quakers, Waterhouse is especially known for his designs for Manchester Town Hall and London's Natural History Museum. The 330-roomed hotel closed in 1933 during the Depression era and, surprisingly for such a fine building, lay empty and unused for over 60 years. It was acquired in 1994 by the John Moores University and converted to accommodate its students as a hall of residence in 1996. Let us hope that they appreciate the grandeur of the building's towers, cornices and Doric pillars.

Right: Large numbers of wealthy merchants set up home around Sefton Park and sent their agents to do business in the Exchange Buildings. There have been several incarnations of the Exchange. The first was one created by James Wyatt in 1808. A more intricately designed building, the work of Matear and Simon, replaced it in 1906. As we can see, it had a remarkable Baroque style façade with statues, raised reliefs and impressive towers. The frontage onto Old Hall Street was replaced by one created in a modern style in the late 1960s and the old main hall replaced by a courtyard.

Below: The city's Town Hall is a great example of Georgian decoration and contains some of the most handsome civic rooms to be found anywhere in the country. The first recorded existence of a town hall in Liverpool makes reference in 1515 to a thatched building serving as such. This was replaced in 1673 by a more substantial one that also acted as an exchange where merchants and traders could do business. The next replacement was built to a design by John Wood the Elder in the middle of the 18th century. An extension to the north, styled by James Wyatt, was added in 1785. This same architect was largely responsible for rebuilding the hall and adding its dome after a calamitous fire in 1795. Some further modification took place in the next century and restoration work was necessitated after bomb damage in 1941.

Seen in panoramas from either side of the last war, Sefton Park rightly has pride of place among our city's open public areas. The thoughts of a nuclear holocaust were very real in most people's minds and the news that another conflict was kicking off over in Korea did little to calm their fears. At least there were times when we found that we could escape our cares and worries, as the young woman above discovered as she gazed out across the calm waters. In the companion picture we can see the Jolly Roger, Captain Hook's vessel. This was really a lifeboat that once belonged to the Cunard fleet. With added masts and sails, it arrived as part of the 1928 Peter Pan pageant. George Audley, a local businessman, donated to Sefton a copy of the statue in London's Kensington Gardens of the boy who never grew up. It was unveiled by a niece of JM Barrie. There was also a model of Wendy's hut and a pair of small cannons. The pirate ship was a delight for children aged from five to ninety-five and was so well loved that it was replaced several times as Mother Nature took her toll. Only the Peter Pan statue now remains, re-sited in the grounds of the Palm House.

It was not until 1816 that any building of significance appeared in a district named Crosby Seabank that was nearly all sandhills and dunes. Since this was the year after one of the most decisive battles of the Napoleonic Wars was fought, the hotel built close to the shore was called the Royal Waterloo. The name of what was really that of a Belgian town began to be used to represent the locality and the practice was formalised when Waterloo became an urban district. The hotel is still there on Marine Terrace, simply known now as the Royal. Tucked away between College Road and Somerville Road, near Merchant Taylors' School, we can find Victoria Park. Wildflower fields as well as more formal flower beds are attractive features here.

Facing page: When John Ryle was appointed as the first Anglican Bishop of Liverpool, the diocese did not have a Cathedral. It used St Peter's Church as a headquarters, but this building was unsatisfactory for upgrading, being far too small. Eventually, after Ryle was succeeded by Francis Chavasse in 1900, consideration was given to building a suitable Cathedral. The design was entrusted to the young Giles Gilbert Scott, son of the architect of the Albert Memorial in London. Giles would also find further fame by introducing red telephone boxes on our streets. The first part of Liverpool Cathedral was consecrated in 1910, but the building had still not been fully completed when it was damaged by enemy action in an air raid in 1940.

Below: The Empire Theatre opened on 9 March, 1925, with a production of 'Better Days', starring Stanley Lupino, Maisie Gay and Ruth French. It was designed by W. and T. R. Milburn and was built by Moss Empires on the site of the former New Prince of Wales Theatre and Opera House which opened in 1866 and at the time was Liverpool's largest theatre. But it was only about three-quarters of the size of the existing Empire and was lit by gas and all the stage machinery was controlled by steam power. Within a year it was renamed the Royal Alexandra Theatre and Opera House to honour the Princess of Wales. The Empire Theatre that stands today was entirely rebuilt and enlarged in 1925 to become the most up-to-date theatre in the provinces. It had the widest auditorium in Europe, and with seating capacity of 2,381 is the largest two-tier theatre in the country.

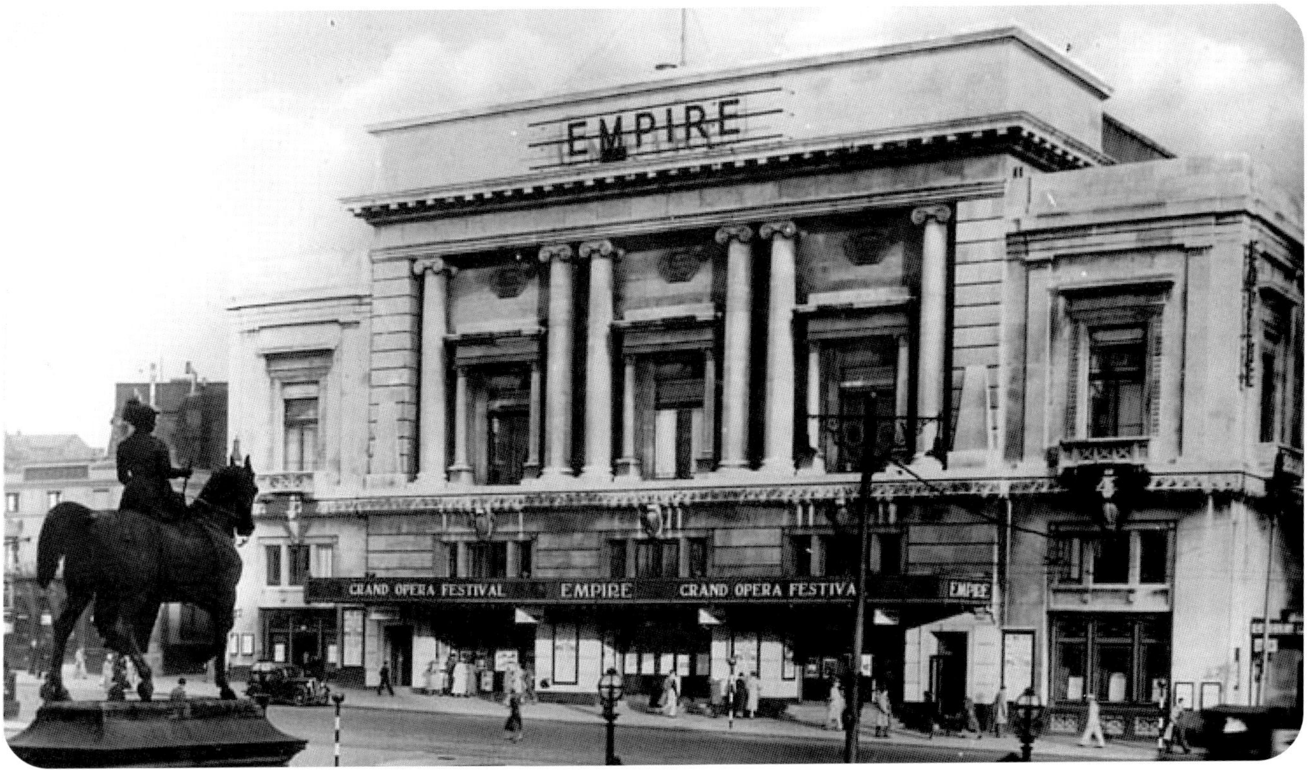

The arrival of "talkies" in 1928 had a positive effect on British film production and cinema going. While film production reached an all-time high in 1936, the 'golden age' of British cinema is usually thought to have occurred in the 1940s. Liverpool itself has an illustrious cinema history, with generations of Merseyside families who grew up watching films at the old picture palaces. The grand old cinemas boasted Art Deco styling, plush seats and the ice cream ladies who appeared in the intermission to sell refreshments. Back in the heyday of popular mass entertainment, Merseyside could boast more than 70 cinema venues. In the following pages we can see just a small selection to help rekindle memories of those wonderful experiences.

This photograph of the Astoria on Walton Road, at the corner of Furness Street, will bring back many memories especially for those readers located in the Walton district of Liverpool. It opened on 21 July, 1930 with Maurice Chevalier in "Innocents of Paris". Showing at the time of this photograph from 1951 was the film 'Storm Warning' with a star-studded cast that included, Doris Day, Ginger Rogers and Ronald Reagan as a District Attorney trying to bring the KKK to justice. The cinema was re-named ABC in December 1963, and was closed in 1974. Many years later, it became a bingo club. This was closed in 2001 when a new purpose built bingo club was built nearby and it was demolished.

Formerly the Picture House, on Lime Street, this cinema's name was changed to the 'Futurist' in 1920, originally having opened in 1912. The Lime Street Picture House was a very upmarket city centre cinema with a tiled Edwardian facade and over a thousand seats. The Futurist Cinema was very popular and managed to retain its hold even after competition from the huge Paramount (Odeon) and Forum (ABC) opened which sometimes forced the Futurist into taking off-circuit films. In May 1954 Twentieth Century Fox took over the cinema as their Cinemascope venue in the city and it was equipped with a large screen. This was a real treat to the local Liverpool girls, as Tyrone Power starred in 'King of the Khyber Rifles' and later, Victor Mature in 'Demetrius and the Gladiator'. Later, in 1960, the Futurist Cinema was acquired by ABC.

This could well be an image of the final days of the Majestic Cinema from 1970, when the cinema was to close. The last films to show were, Alfred Hitchcock's "The Birds" and Howard Keel in "The Day of the Triffids". This brought to an end over 55 years of cinema going on this site, although the original Majestic Picture House of 1914, was demolished in 1937 and the building we see in the photograph was built to replace it. Located in the east of the inner city centre at the corner of Daulby Street and Prescott Street, the magnificent corner entrance was dominated by a slender fin 75 feet high tower feature, which had the Majestic named vertically placed. The site is now part of the grounds of The Royal Liverpool University Hospital.

Right: Located on Lime Street, adjacent to the 1912 built Lime Street Picture House/Futurist Cinema. The Scala Super Cinema was opened on 16 January, 1916. In 1920, a new company was formed and the Scala and Futurist came under the same ownership. The Scala Super Cinema screened its first talkie on 8 July, 1929. In the mid-1950s and 60s, the Scala Cinema screened mainly second run films together with 'X' certificate films. It continued the adult film policy under independent management until taken over by ABC in July 1967. It continued as a cinema until August 1982 when it closed. It stood empty for several years, until 1987, when it was transformed into a nightclub, known as the Hippodrome.

Below: The ABC Granada was located on the corner of Lime Street in the Dovecot district east of Liverpool. The Cinema was opened on 24 December, 1932 with "The Rosery". It was designed in an Art Deco style by Liverpool based architect Ernest Shennan. Associated British Cinemas(ABC) took over the cinema in 1935 and continued showing the latest movies until its closure in 1961. Subsequently it was converted into a Granada Bingo Club as we can see here in this photograph. Later operated as a Mecca Bingo Club, which eventually closed in 1994.

Most visitors to Liverpool who have left their train at Lime Street Station will recognise this building as it would be their first sight as they left the station. It is a grand, Grade II listed building formerly known as the Forum. It was acquired by ABC in 1930 and with its six-storey interior, became one of the finest cinemas in the area. It was a single screen cinema until 1982 when 3 screens were installed and in 1986 it changed its name to the Cannon which helped it to survive until 1998. 'James T Kirk' and 'Spock' were the main attractions for the fine building when this photograph was take in 1982, as the blockbuster, 'Star Trek II- The Wrath of Khan' had come to Liverpool which would hopefully bring in the cinemagoers. Sadly, the building finally closed in January 1998 and remains unused.

THE LANDING STAGE

This is a very early scene of Liverpool's famous 'Princes Landing Stage' and dates from the turn of the last century. It was busy with the travellers of the time, smart men in Bowler hats, Homburgs and flat caps, ladies in long dresses and small children showing off their Sunday best. It was a popular transit point and the steam boats, laden with passengers and cargo would cross from here to Ireland and further afield. To account for the large tidal surges on the Mersey, the Landing Stage was designed to float so passengers could embark and disembark regardless of the time of day. Cargo ships had to use the enclosed docks to load and unload their cargo due to its size and weight.

Left: Another two stacked steamer is carefully manoeuvred into position along Liverpool's Landing Stage by a small tug boat around 1910. The hustle and bustle suggests a busy weekend, with horse and carts delivering and collecting passengers, stevedores man handling cargo onto trucks and hand carts and officials trying their best to keep everything moving smoothly. You may just be able to make out the wagon near the waterfront on the left, which is laden with barrels, these are most likely full of imported liquor which would be well received by inhabitants and visitors alike, across Liverpool.

Below: A very pretty and engaging photo at first glance of a shopkeeper standing in the doorway of her shop in Penny Lane, Liverpool. But the hoardings to the right tell of a major tragedy which would have been particularly poignant for the people of Liverpool and their affinity with the sea. It was the year the great ship the Titanic had hit an iceberg and the unthinkable had occurred. It was April 1912 when the local newspapers, the Daily Sketch, Daily Mail, Daily Despatch and Daily News told the story of that great disaster. The RMS Titanic was on her way from Southampton to New York on her maiden voyage. None of the 1684 passengers reported to have drowned by the Daily Post hoarding would have dreamt such a catastrophe would occur to a ship previously glorified for its 'unsinkability'. The lady at Burton House stationers would have taken no pleasure in selling many newspapers to those on their way to the Landing Stage would have, no doubt, taken time to consider and mourn the loss.

Above: This is a very unusual photo of Liverpool docks. It was taken in the wartime of the 1940s and shows a Minesweeping Flotilla moored in the docks. Liverpool had become a major naval base for Britain during WWII with a significant focus on the 'battle for the Atlantic'. Because of this the the city and its docks sustained persistent bombing raids by the Germans, 68 in total which was the most of any port outside London. There was more than 1285 convoys of ships which visited Liverpool docks during the war years and with some of these containing more than 60 individual ships, the work for the dock hands, labourers and tug boats was immense. It wasn't just the docks that were targeted, tens of thousands of homes were destroyed in the bombing raids and over 180,000 heavily damaged. Over 4,000 people were killed and more than 4,000 were seriously injured. The naval escort ships, pictured here, were a vital protection to ensure cargo ships could continue to bring goods and cargo to the UK and transport armed forces and munitions away.

Top right: It hardly needs to be said that this was the age of steam. The small but powerful tug boat blows out a white plume of steam from its whistle stack to warn of its arrival and a heavier darker cloud from its chugging engines, whilst the ship being pulled needs only a puff of black smoke as its work is almost over. Positioning these large vessels under steam power in the 1930s was no easy feat. The docks at Liverpool well enclosed and allocated berths to offload a variety of cargos could, at times, be difficult to access. Dock workers can be seen behind the steam and smoke on both sides of the quay, no doubt getting ready for the tough and heavy days work.

Right: This aerial view of Princes Dock shows one of the enclosed dock areas where ships would moor and unload their cargos. It was an intricate mix of roads, waterways, moorings and sheds, situated in the heart of the city and encompassing the famous Liver Building. The high level view shows clearly how the relatively small tug boats help to manoeuvre the large ship to its final position against the dock side.

The great ships which visited Liverpool, and there were many, have their own individual stories to tell and the following photographs will evoke memories of grand parents telling of famous names and the excitement of the city when the arrival of a particular ship was announced.

Above: The RMS Lusitania was the largest passenger liner of its time and owned by the Cunard Line. Launched in 1906 with its 4 great funnels, it had six decks and four propellers to reach a top speed of 26 knots. This photo was taken in 1911 with the liner moored at the Liverpool Landing Stage whilst an overcrowded ferry boat chugs its way to New Brighton across the Mersey. There was no expectation of war at this time and people would go about their business normally with the lucky few boarding the world's largest liner to take them to new lives across the world. It was 1 May, 1915, when the great Lusitania would leave New York for Liverpool for the last time. German U Boats would torpedo the ship on 7 May just off the coast of Ireland, a second internal explosion would see the ship sink to the bottom of the ocean in just 18 minutes. Passengers and crew numbering 1,198 were lost in this tragic end to one of the great ships of the 20th century.

Below: AnotherCunard liner shown just off Liverpool docks in 1914 is the RMS Aquitania. The sister ship to the Lusitania and Mauritania, she survived two world wars and returned to passenger service after both occasions. Built on Clydebank, in Scotland, and launched in 1913, she became the longest service passenger liner until the QEII took that crown in 2004. This grand photo of one of the worlds best loved liners set against the equally loved Liver Building gives a nostalgic view of Britain's world leading construction and engineering capabilities of the time.

Right: At the Landing Stage is the RMS Adriatic, a ship not quite as grand as the Cunard liners but one still which would steam across the Atlantic in a time when passenger air travel still a long way to go. Launched in 1906 by Harland & Wolf, she belonged to the White Star Line and was the first ship to have an indoor swimming pool and Turkish Bath. The ship was finally scrapped in Japan, in 1935.

Below: This sea going giant which should need no introduction is the massive aircraft carrier, HMS Ark Royal. However, this is not the one we will have seen recently on the TV being decommissioned in 2011. The ship in this photo is the aircraft carrier built by Cammell Laird, of Birkenhead, on launch day, 13 April, 1937. It was a huge 800ft-long vessel and had a range of 8,700 miles carrying a crew of 1,580 officers and sailors. Sadly, a desperate fate also awaited this fine ship and after an illustrious life in many of the major conflict zones of WWII, the ship was torpedoed by a German U Boat on 13 November, 1941, just off the coast of Gibraltar, an unbefitting end to such a proud ship and its crew.

REFRESH TS

Left: Built in Belgium in 1922, The SS Empire Test started live as a passenger liner named the 'Thysville'. It was a modest liner of the time and was later taken over by the British Ministry of War Transport during the Second World War. This ship joined forces with many other similar frigates and small passenger ships, all of which were renamed with the prefix of 'Empire'. The SS Empire Test was used to evacuate British citizens from Egypt and played a number of supporting roles moving armed forces personnel from Liverpool to the ports of Europe. It is pictured here around 1950 at the Landing Stage only three years before it was scrapped in Scotland.

Above: Another photo from the 1950s shows the Landing Stage from a different perspective. The many double decker buses of the time are lined up at their allocated stops and would have looked very grand in their colour scheme of red with a green stripe or cream with a green stripe. The 19 buses in this shot don't seem to be heavily used given the number of tourists and travellers in the photo, but maybe they have all just boarded and others from across the Mersey are waiting to alight.

WHEN WE WERE YOUNG

Below: These boys look very studious at Merchant Taylors' School, Crosby, in the early 1900s. It was the Drawing Room at the school and we can see from the blackboard just behind the teacher, that this was no 'flowers and landscapes' class. The geometric shapes on the board and in the middle of the floor, suggest that this was more of a technical drawing class where cones and cubes had to be accurately transposed onto paper with correct angles and proportions and, of course, Merchant Taylors' School would expect nothing less.

Right: There's not much room left for children to watch the Punch and Judy Show in St Georges Place, in 1905. The adults seem to have taken up the viewing area on the cobbled street. It may have been that a few lucky children were sat at the front and looking up at the antics of the crocodile, villain and policeman as the show went on. Punch and Judy has its roots in 16th century Italy, with Punch originally known as 'Puncinella'. Adapted and built on from accepted myths and stories, it has lasted well as a popular children's entertainment.

Below: It look's as if 'schools out' for these kids, or maybe it hasn't yet started. They are all over the Steble Fountain in William Brown Street in the 1930s. The fountain was named after a Mayor of Liverpool in the mid 19th century and stands just across from Wellingtons Column. These little ones seem to be just enjoying the water and splashing around, but the girl in the centre will need to be careful to make sure her large teddy bear doesn't get wet. The others on the steps of the column still look to be barefoot so maybe the little chap at the front is picking up his older brothers boots to take them over to him.

Above: Fitness and exercise is all the fashion these days, but in the 1930s and 1940s knowledge about health and exercise was still in its infancy. Given the food available to many and the manual labour for both working men and housewives, obesity was generally not a problem. However, at Liverpool University's Walter Harding Gymnasium these students were being taken through a series of exercises which would hopefully keep them healthy and provide a basis for exercise throughout their lives. The Walter Harding Gym was replaced by a new sports centre and pool in 1966 and several Olympians and Para-Olympians would achieve great things following their time at Liverpool.

Right: These amphibious vehicles known as 'ducks' were a popular attraction on the beaches of New Brighton and would always excite the children. Of course, the vehicles were not designed as a beach ride, but more for the armed forces which provided a land vehicle with sea-going capabilities. It was an American design and proved popular with the soldiers and seamen who used them. This photo from 1946 certainly gives the impression that the 'duck' would beat the 'donkeys' for most kids.

Above: Christmas in the hospital didn't have to be all bad and these children who would have surely believed in Santa in these much more innocent days. They would have been thrilled to have a visit from such a loved character. He was in fact the deliverer of presents funded by the 'Christmas Treat Fund' which had been established locally to provide for children in hospitals and orphanages around Liverpool. If there was anything left over after Christmas, those children luck enough, may be taken to the cinema or to sports days as a special treat.

Below: It was a wonderful day out at Wilkies Mammoth Circus, in New Brighton, for this happy family in the 1950s. The little girl will have been thrilled to see the lions and tigers with their courageous handler, the fancy horses parading around the ring and trotting to music from the circus band. She may have even dared to think of the high wire act and the dangerous balancing acts whilst juggling. The whole family will have laughed at the clowns and their antics with pies in the face and buckets of 'fake water' being thrown into the crowd. These are the memories which live with us all through our lives and are so precious to us over the years.

Right: The little lad looks puzzled at the lady with the big hat, but of course this was just her washing day bundle that she conveniently carried on her head. He is supporting a bobby dazzler of a haircut himself. Common at the time, the 'bowl cut' was achieved by putting a cooking pot over the head and shaving off the hair below the rim. This was the time before hot running water and washing machines in many houses, so this lady's job may well have been to take neighbours large sheets and pillow cases to the local steam laundry, for a small charge, no doubt.

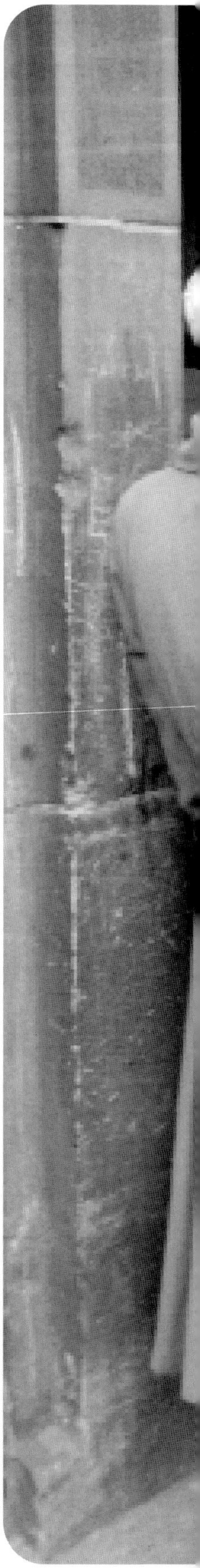

Left: Who says school days couldn't be fun? These girls certainly thought so and they were new Year 1 pupils at the Merchant Taylors' Junior School, in Stanfield. The girls were asked to climb on this wooden frame for a picture in 1953. They were very smart in their school uniforms but we have to ask if they would have been allowed to clamber to the top of this frame in today's world of Health & Safety restrictions. Merchant Taylors' School Girls school started in 1888 with just 12 pupils, it now has over 600 who, no doubt, are having as much fun as the ones in the picture.

Above: You would be the envy of all your friends if you were luck enough to get a Hornby Train set for Christmas and by the look of these children's faces in 1954, at the English Electric Show, it would be top of their list too. The parents looking on would probably already know this set was out of their reach but would let the kids dream a little. Watching the accurate replica engines and carriages run around the track, under bridges and past perfect little stations would keep their attention for a good while, at least until the next best toy hit the high streets, possibly a Scalextric.

GETTING ABOUT

Above: The patience of this gentleman angler is shown in this 1907 photo on the Leeds, Liverpool canal, although he probably only needed to step back from the bank once or twice a day. It's unlikely an angler in today's fishing circles would be seen pipe smoking in 'plus fours'! The heavy barge pulled by the single shire horse would have been a common sight in those days and whilst the woman guiding the horse looks a little weary, the horse itself seems to be enjoying lunch from a galvanised tin bucket. Heavy barges carrying cargo from Liverpool to Leeds and all points in-between were a popular mode of transport for bulk goods with a well maintained canal system providing the route. Although it was a much slower pace, the only real costs were for food for the horse itself and wages for the barge hands.

Right: The scene of progress show a steam tractor along side several heavy horses. Clearly, Aldersons Removal Contractors had decided that steam power was better than the horse power which would have served them so well in the past. The photograph shows the transporting of beef from the SS Baltic at the dockside and horses covered with sacks, possibly against the cold, as they tuck into a well earned feed from the nose bags attached to their harnesses. It was a typical haulage scene and similar transport would develop over the coming years.

Below: The ships funnel on the far left confirms this is the riverside railway station in the early part of last century. Horse-drawn taxis await the ships passengers and the young handler at the front is waiting patiently for the next fare. The sign writing on the side of the front carriage shows it belongs to the White Star Line, one of the major passenger shipping companys of the day. Founded in Liverpool in 1845, it merged with the Cunard Line in 1934 and operated as the 'Cunard-White Star Line' until 1950. It is unlikely that the horse-drawn carriages would have lasted much longer given the pace of change in many forms of transport.

It is a similar scene of progress at the gates of the Henry Tate's Sugar Refinery, in Liverpool, with raw sugar entering the gates and crystal sugar being taken for distribution on the back of an early motor wagon. The horses and carts lined up in the photo stand quietly in pairs waiting for the photographer to take his shot before they set off to local outlets. The carts are heavily laden, requiring two heavy horses for each job. During the construction of the Love Lane Refinery in the early 1870s, Henry Tate adapted the plans to incorporate a new refining technique to increase the yield of white sugar. When the refinery became operational in 1872, it produced 400 tons of sugar a week.

Above: The Prince of Wales visited Liverpool on 2 July, 1921 ,and one of his royal duties was to open the Hall of Remembrance in recognition of the 13,000 Liverpool men who lost their lives in WW1. The Prince is seen here, looking more like a 'passer-by' admiring the fine car parked on a Liverpool street, than a crowned Prince who was about to be chauffeured to his next official engagement. A slight give-away is the gent in the striped suit behind the Prince who has 'doffed' his bowler hat, as one would, in the presence of royalty. The car, possibly a Rolls Royce Silver Ghost convertible, heads up a cavalcade of other fine motors of the time as would befit a visiting royal party.

Left: Trains will always feature in any story about Liverpool, they were, along with the ships, a significant part of the city and its growth to greater prosperity. The Liverpool and Manchester Railway opened in 1830 and was the first one to rely solely on steam power with no horse-drawn carriages. Steam power is still evident in this photograph form the mid-1940s. Here we see an English news girl selling newspapers to American soldiers on their way to Southampton.

The Liverpool Overhead Railway opened in 1893 and mainly serviced the dock area of the city. It was the first electric elevated railway in the world and used electric lights and signalling. The line was extended northwards to Seaforth Sands on 30 April 1894. An extension southwards from Herculaneum Dock to Dingle was opened on 21 December, 1896. During World War II, the railway suffered extensively from bomb damage.The railway is featured in the film Waterfront (1950) and in the final scenes of the film The Clouded Yellow (1951), as the character played by Jean Simmons uses it to travel to one of the docks. Demolition of the structure commenced in September 1957, completed the following year. The motor coaches were built in Birmingham and most would be used throughout the 63-year life of the railway, which closed in 1956 due to the cost of refurbishing many of the viaducts and overhead structures. The railway had served the local community well over the years and was known locally as the 'Dockers Umbrella' as many dock workers would walk beneath it on their way from dock to dock, sheltering from the rain.

VAUXHALL

14
12

Left: You could imagine the noise levels would be quite high as these nine trams in shot rattle backwards and forwards along Church Street in this busy scene. For some of our older readers, the sight of these mechanical monsters will bring back fond memories, even though the ride might not have been that special at the time. Electric trams first operated in Liverpool in November 1898. With the ability to carry 48 passengers upstairs and down, the new railed transport had nearly double the capacity of the old horse trams. At the height of the tram operation in 1945 there were 744 trams running in Liverpool along 63 routes. Trams at this time outnumbered buses three to one. Following the Second World War, Liverpool City Council took the decision to move away from trams in favour of buses. From 1948 onwards the network was wound down with the last trams running in 1957.

Top and above: An earlier form of public transport shows the open top version of a Liverpool tram, some 15 years earlier. The uniformed driver and 'clippy' are admired by the two lads to the right who dressed typically in their flat caps and scarves. However, it wasn't long before the motorised omnibus began to be seen on the streets of Liverpool and here we see a 1927 Karrier WL6/2 with its sign for Aigburth, an affluent suburb to the south of the city.

A tunnel under the Mersey had been proposed as far back as 1825 and again in 1914, the latter proposals being halted due to the outbreak of war. Finally, the project was authorised to go ahead in 1925. The immense boring machine was started by Princess Mary with the turning of a golden key on 16 December, 1925. Tunnelling was carried out from both sides of the Mersey, with the 2 tunnels being joined in 1928. We can see from the early photos the huge scale of this project which was unprecedented in engineering terms at the time.

The opening ceremony warranted a dignitary of no less standing than the King himself, King George V, visiting Liverpool on 18 July, 1934, to perform the grand opening ceremony. Over 200,000 people gathered to watch the ceremony.

At just over 2 miles in length, the tunnel was the longest underwater tunnel in the world for over 24 years. It had two branch tunnels on either side of the river to access the docks areas. The one in the direction of Birkenhead closed in 1965. The tunnel soon became a popular transport route across the Mersey with car drivers happy to pay the tolls required for its upkeep.

CAMBRIAN

BRITISH EUROPEAN AIRWAYS
G-AGZD

Facing page: As the years progressed and the city grew, the needs for faster travel across Europe and beyond grew with it. Speke Airport was opened in the grounds of Speke Hall, in 1933, with a growing demand for flights to Ireland, initially. The airport began to grow steadily until the RAF took control, in 1940, with Speke then playing a vital role during the war years as not only a take-off and landing point but also a crucial aeroplane building facility using the shadow factory nearby. 1945 saw the return to normal civilian operations and passenger number grew further, outstripping the local competitor airport of Manchester. The city of Liverpool would take control of the airport in 1961, with ambitious development plans and a new runway was subsequently opened by Prince Phillip, in 1966. The original control tower seen in these photos, built in the 1930s, was left derelict for over 10 years as a new terminal building had been built, however, it has now been refurbished and become part of a hotel complex. The re-naming of the airport in 2001 to the 'Liverpool John Lennon Airport' was well received and further consolidated its position as a major global airport destination.

Above: Coaches, double-deckers, single-deckers, cars and pedestrians, it all looks a bit chaotic at the Hood Street Gyratory, Liverpool in 1985. It was probably not surprising at the time as it was the busiest bus terminus in Liverpool. If you have a look at the roofing above each of the stops you will be able to guess why the stops became known as the 'bubble bus stops'. Happily, the chaos has now been sorted out in what is now known as Queens Square.

THE POST-WAR YEARS

This delightful collection of photographic memories will appeal to all who grew up in this post-war decade. They include pictures of children enjoying life out on the streets, at home and at school, on holiday and at memorable events in the Liverpool area. These wonderful period pictures and captions will bring back childhood memories and help to reflect our thoughts on aspects of life as it was in post-war Britain.

On 8 May, 1945, the Second World War ended in Europe, but rationing continued. Some aspects of rationing became even stricter for some years after the war. Many people expected rationing to be lifted as soon as peace was declared, but it was nine years until the last ration book was issued. After years of war, continued rationing was a terrible blow. Proud men who had fought their way from Normandy to Germany came back to find themselves with no home of their own, living in squalid lets or forced to lodge with in-laws. Home life was also hard to come to terms with after years away. Wives and children might resent the returning 'stranger' back from the war.

Despite the hardship, there remained resilience, humour and a sense of fun. People who had become accustomed to little were content with simple things. Cinema, sport and radio, combined with 'holidays at home' or the British seaside and Butlin's camps, were the entertainment, there being little travel abroad. Since people did not have TV, going to the cinema was very popular. Most people went to the cinema at least once a week and many people went twice.

The National Health Service started in 1948 in a society weary but disciplined by war, and accustomed to austerity. There was a school dental service and a special priority service for expectant and nursing mothers and young children. A major innovation, health centres in the community, had been planned but few were built.

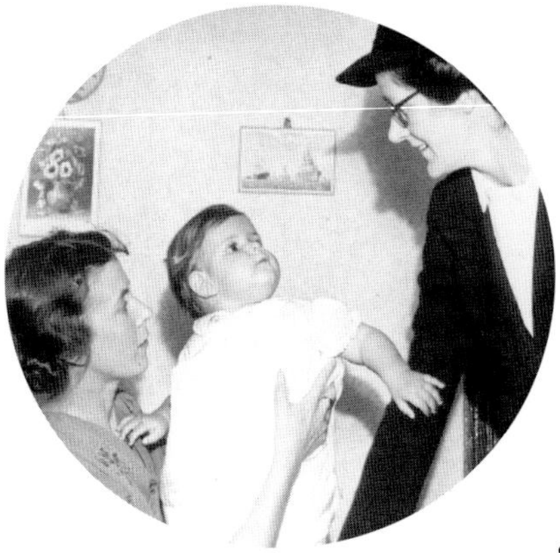

In 1951 the Festival of Britain provided a glimpse of a better future. It was a national exhibition held throughout the UK in the summer of 1951. It was organised by the government to give the British a feeling of recovery in the aftermath of war and to promote the British contribution to science, technology, industrial design, architecture and the arts. The Festival's centrepiece was in London on the South Bank of the Thames.

Children of the 50s have much to look back on with fondness: Muffin the Mule, Andy Pandy and Dennis the Menace became part of the family for many.

The railway platform was a another popular haven away from the watchful eyes of parents. It's hard to imagine today that we lived in a country where doors were left unlocked, children played safely in the street and people really did look out for each other.

The post-war welfare state offered free orange juice, milk and healthcare, and there was lots to do, whether football in the street, a double bill at the cinema, a game of tiddly-winks or a spot of roller-skating. The purple stains of iodine on the knees of boys in short trousers and knitted bathing costumes bring back fond and sometimes painful memories from over 60 years ago. But for those born around then, this era of childhood feels like yesterday. Children's bedrooms were completely different; no TV, no PC, no Games Console and no massive stacks of toys. All you had were a few books and some toys, all of which would be tidied up before you went to bed.

It was an era of innovation in toys, just as much as in other fields. However, traditional roles were still re-enforced.

Boys have always played with toy cars, trains and guns, and girls played at homemaking with dolls. Traditional boys toys like Meccano and Dinky cars were still firm favourites, but they were joined by new rivals Matchbox and Corgi.

However, when Fred Francis gave his already popular Scalex cars an electric motor and a track with a groove instead of a rail, the definitive slot racing game Scalectrix was born. Young lads would look in the toyshop window, hoping and praying that father Christmas would look on their good deeds favourably and deliver a set at Christmas.

Dolls and dolls' houses were still firm favourites with girls They also had play washing lines and toy cups and saucers. Topics popular on television and the cinema influenced play in the 50s.

Popular children's TV programmes such as the Flower Pot Men and Muffin the Mule spawned toy replicas and the best selling toy of 1954 was Sooty's Xylophone.

Anything from the Wild West, from cap guns to Cowboy and Indian outfits, was popular. Science fiction also influenced toys, introducing children to a world of ray guns and robots. With a constant diet of war films on the cinema and TV, the Second World War was also a popular theme. Football was just as popular with 50s boys as it is today. They could enjoy playing soccer indoors when the classic football game Subbuteo was first marketed in 1947.

Everyone who grew up in fifties Britain will have his or her own indelible memories of their childhood, from the first taste of welfare orange juice to the birth of rock' n' roll. The nation was recovering from the ravages of the war and the camaraderie of wartime was still evident throughout the country. But it didn't matter if you had no television because you could play in the streets without the fear of traffic or the obstruction of parked cars.

Buses and bicycles were the most popular modes of transport. In 1950, there were just under two million cars in Britain, with only 14 per cent of households owning one.

The 1950s house was a working house and in the early part of the decade, many homes still did not have bathrooms and only had outside lavatories as in the above picture. With no bathroom the choice would be either to wash in a tin bath by the fireside or take a weekly trip to the local municipal baths where they could pay to have a hot bath in a little more comfort.

Boys and girls played street games together, such as run outs, hopscotch and British bulldog.

In the playground schoolgirls practiced handstands and cartwheels with their skirts tucked up under the elastic of their navy blue knickers, while the boys played conkers.

Dusty, old-fashioned sweet shops had high wooden counters jam-packed with boxes of ha'penny chews and other sweet delights. Remember Lucky Bags and frozen Jubblys and getting a sore tongue from sucking on gobstoppers, aniseed balls and Spangles? Then there were those old Smith's potato crisps. The salt was in a twist of blue paper and you always had to rummage around for it at the bottom of the bag.

For many children the spending time at the fair during wakes was their holiday, and they loved it.

The housing situation greatly improved in the late 1950s and 1960s when large-scale slum clearance took place when whole swathes of old terraced houses were demolished. High-rise flats replaced some of them.

As the years went on TV grew in popularity, the home slowly developed more into the entertainment mould. Sitting Room chairs would be turned to face the TV rather than the fire and generations of the same family would gather together to watch specific TV programmes.

At the start of the 'Swinging Sixties', life was on the move, for most it was a move upwards. Things which in the 1950s were seen as extravagant were now starting to be seen as expected. This led to a lifestyle which was evolved around leisure. With more and more people buying cars, the population became more mobile.

In the home, interior design was reflecting the revolution in music and entertainment with bright floral patterns all the rage. There was growth in British fashion, cinema and popular music. The centre of the sitting room, now called the 'lounge', was the TV set and stereo system (late 60s).

There was greater trust and neighbourliness in the Sixties. Families did more together and there was a greater sense of family values. Growing up was a time where school, home, and play life taught children discipline but allowed them to have fun and experience life safe environment. For many children, the 60s were considered the 'Age of Innocence'. For instance, kids got to go to the movies to watch westerns like, The Magnificent Seven, The Good the Bad and the Ugly and Butch Cassidy and the Sundance Kid. They were able to play with their friends in a field or the woods after school. You could play out until it got dark and your mum would shout you in to come and get your tea.

With more and more cars on the road, the National Cycling Proficiency Scheme was introduced by the Government in 1958. The first child to get 100% for this test was Stephen Borrill of Scunthorpe in 1962 and was featured on the front page of the 'The News of the World'.

Even the most shocking fashions were popularised in the 1960s by models who, for the first time became superstars, like Jean Shrimpton and Twiggy. The miniskirt was the fashion phenomenon of the Sixties, hemlines rose to seven or eight inches above the knee. One of the first places to sell them was Mary Quants King's Road boutique, 'Bazaar', in London in 1965. Music also played a part with the Beatles in Liverpool and a mix of bands including The Who, The Kinks and The Rolling Stones who went on to worldwide success.

An icon of the 1960s, the Morris Mini

Scooters like those outside Geneva Motors on Renshaw Street in the image below were a common sight in the 1960s. This form of transport was popular with students and modernists which was shortened to 'mods'. They collected music by the Small Faces, washed their hair and often wore long duffel coats. Their sworn enemies were the greasy bikers who still clung to the songs of Gene Vincent and Johnny Kidd. Known as 'rockers', they had connections with the later motorcycle gangs of Hell's Angels.

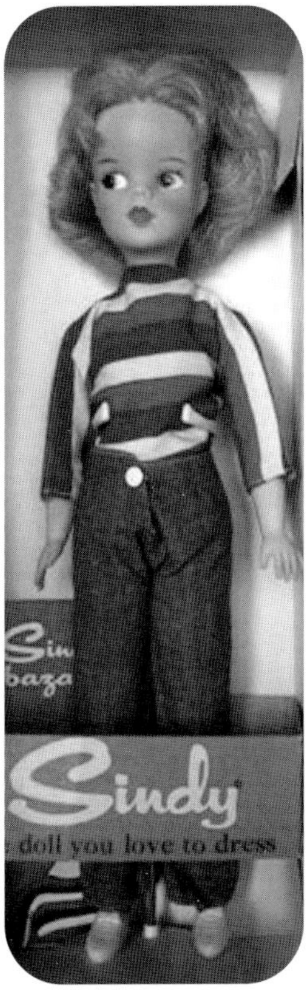

Playtime in the 60s was about innovation and tradition. Whilst traditional roles remained with girls doing pretend housework and boys still playing soldiers, science fiction gave way to the real space race and the inventiveness and freedom of the 60s brought new ways for children to play. The 60s was also a decade for new dolls. The American invader Barbie launched in the late 50s, with Britain's own version, Sindy, arriving in the shops in 1963.

SOME OF THE MOST POPULAR TV SHOWS OF THE 1950S, 1960 & 1970S

1950s

- I Love Lucy
- Robin Hood
- The Gang Show
- The Army Game
- Emergency Ward Ten
- Wagon Train
- Criss Cross Quiz
- The Invisible Man
- William Tell
- The Count of Monte Cristo
- The Four Just Men
- The Flying Doctor

1960s

- Armchair Theatre
- Bootsie & Snudge
- The Larkins
- Steptoe & Son
- Double Your Money
- Stingray
- Coronation Street
- Till Death Us Do Part
- The Avengers
- Thunderbirds
- Danger Man
- The Saint
- In Loving Memory

1970s

- The Pursuaders
- Benny Hill
- This is Your Life
- Opportunity Knocks
- Bless This House
- On The Buses
- The Sweeney
- George & Mildred
- Man About The House
- Mind Your Language
- Sale Of The Century
- To The Manor Born
- Danger Man
- The Saint
- In Loving Memory

For years toymakers thought that boys would not play with dolls, but were proved wrong in the 60s by the sufficiently tough looking soldier called Action Man, which was based on an American toy called GI Joe. The world of secret agents and spies came to the big screen in the 60s with James Bond. Corgi Toys were quick to cash in with a model of Bond's Aston Martin DB5 with a working ejector seat. Corgi introduced a number of cars based on film and TV and overtook Dinky in the toy car industry.

Etch-A-Sketch allowed children to produce detailed blue print-like drawings and shake the toy to rub them out and start again. The original Spirograph caused a sensation when it was launched in 1965.

The 70s started where the 60s left off. Hippy ideas and fashions were becoming part of mainstream culture. In the 70s, everyone wore flares; technological advances brought many improvements to home life and travel abroad became accessible to many more people.

It was the decade of the Space Hopper, the Ford Cortina, Raleigh Chopper bikes, the record player and cassette recorder.

The big new luxury for many people in the 70s was colour television. Nearly all programmes in the 70s were broadcast in colour and more people were able to stretch to afford a colour set. For some the 70s is the golden era of British television with programmes such as Fawlty Towers, Whatever Happened to the Likely Lads and the colour episodes of Dad's Army.

In the early 1970s many Britons finally had the chance to get on the property ladder as the Bank of England relaxed its lending rules. And, although we often think of the 1970s as the end of something - the tired, miserable hangover after the long party of the Swinging Sixties - it makes much more sense to see them as the beginning of a new chapter in the story of modern Britain.

For most ordinary people, after all, the 1970s brought new experiences that their parents and grandparents could barely have imagined. The most obvious example is the package holiday abroad, which 30 years earlier would have seemed like something from science fiction. Even for relatively poor working-class families, holidays no longer meant Blackpool and Bognor but Malta and Majorca.

The first big new sound of the 1970s was 'Glam Rock', the main figures of this were David Bowie, Elton John and of course Gary Glitter. In the bleak political backdrop, these larger that life British bands and characters brought a welcome relief with their platform boots, sequins, nail varnish and colourful hair.

The big change in play in the 70s though was the advent of electronic games. The 70s gave us digital watches and pocket calculators and by the middle of the decade electronic toys and games as well. One of the first to capture the imagination of the UK public was the Atari Video Computer which dominated the home video game market. The brightly coloured MB Simon game was also a big seller in 1978.

Star Wars was in the cinema in 1977 and a host of Star Wars inspired merchandise followed. Never before had the movie makers cashed in so much on the toy market, it was a portent for the new decade.

AT WORK

Below: The working life of women had changed forever following the Great War and was changed even further with the onset of WWII. It was an arduous and dirty job for these women at the Fazakerley Ordnance factory in 1943 as their role was to assemble the various parts of a breech block (the blocks, pins, extractors and springs that are the part of the firearm action that closes the breech of a weapon) with parts that had arrived from all over the country. These women and their colleagues would fill the vast numbers of ordinary jobs left after their men folk had embarked for Europe and beyond and the additional ordnance work in support of the war effort would occupy many more.

Right: These ladies were checking the cases of wireless sets made by English Electric back in 1947. Clothed in their smocks with the almost obligatory head scarf, they would diligently scour the Bakelite cases for any blemishes or cracks, before they were passed to have the electronic valves and components fitted. This type of radio or wireless as it was known would be bought by many families in a time before television became a household item. It was what a family would sit around and listen to the Home Service or Light Entertainment, the two stations at the time. It would be a family affair and everyone had to be quiet for dad when the news came on.

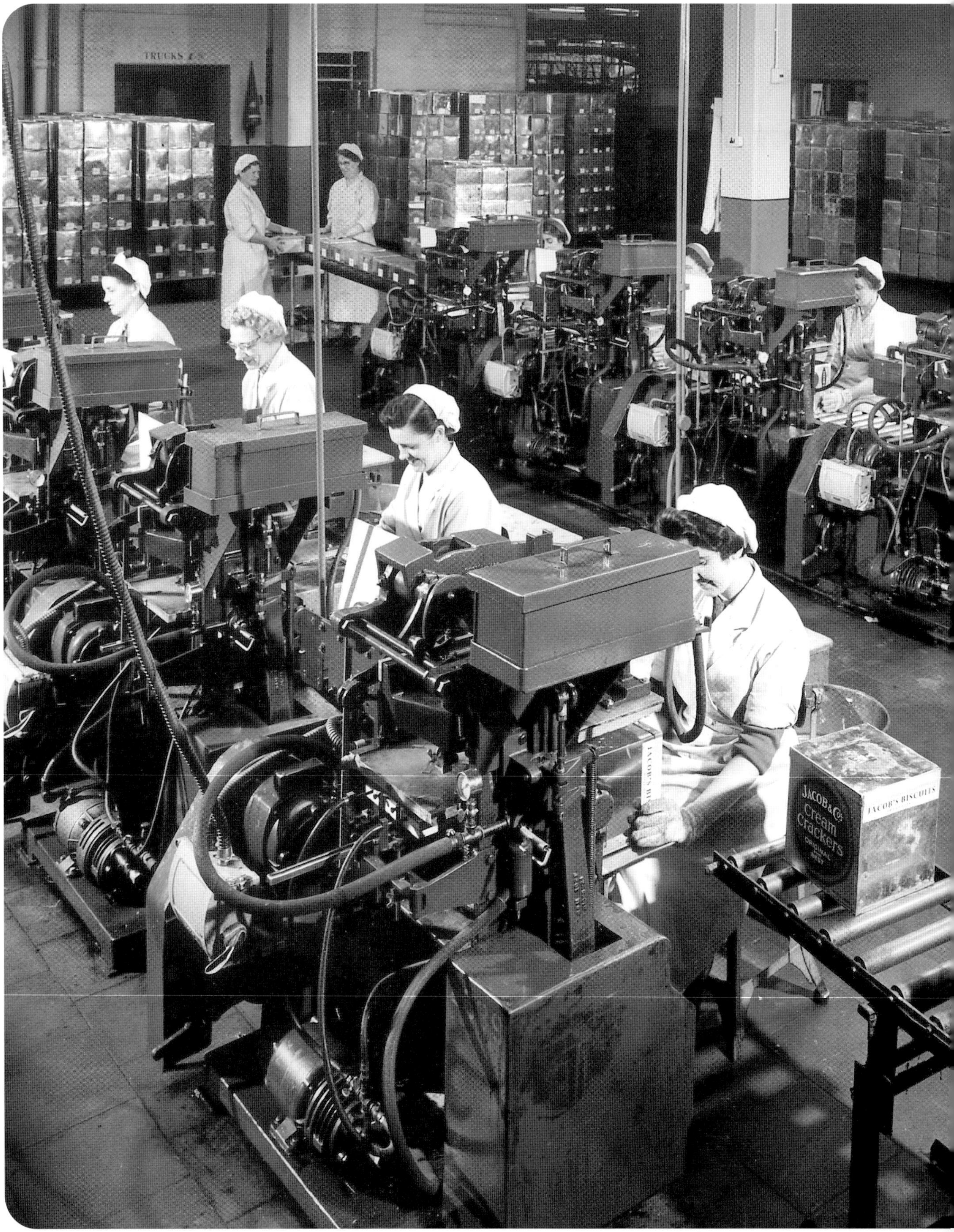
TRUCKS
JACOB & Co's
Cream
Crackers
ORIGINAL
BEST
JACOB'S BISCUITS

Jacobs came to Aintree in 1910 when it was decided there was insufficient space for expansion at its Dublin base and soon the company became famous for its 'Cream Crackers', which had been invented as far back as 1885. The factory produced ration biscuits for the forces during the war and the much loved 'Club Biscuit' was launched just after the war. The fame of Jacobs grew and it soon had a worldwide following for its range of biscuits and crackers. For those of you who love Twiglets, you'll be pleased to know this also became a popular Jacobs brand having originally being launched by Peak Frean as a Christmas treat in 1932. Who'd have thought the simple Twiglet was over 80 years old! The ladies at the packaging machines in the 1960s are boxing Cream Crackers for export.

Dinky toys still have a special place in the heart for many of us and will muster fond memories of playtime with our friends and showing off what new car, coach or lorry we might have been lucky enough to receive as a birthday present. The ladies at the Binns Road plant on the left of the conveyor are packing 'cranes' which you may remember had the arm which could be raised and lowered by turning the handle on the side of the cab, a great addition to any collection. These ladies enjoyed their work, chatting and packing at the same time as listening to light entertainment shows and music broadcast over the tannoy system.

John Mason International

Moving the World

The vans of the removal firm of John Mason International Ltd are amongst the most familiar sights around Liverpool. The firm has been in business for over 130 years. If you aren't old enough to recall removals being made by horse-drawn vehicles there were certainly many members of the Mason family who could.

It was in 1884 that the firm was founded in Wavertree, then on the outskirts of Liverpool, by Mrs Mary Mason. Before starting out on her own Mary had earlier helped her husband John in his carting business. When Mary's son, also John, began helping her in 1887 coal deliveries became the main activity. In 1890, 17-year-old John took over and expanded the business into general haulage. In that same year a contract was signed with a local company that was to last for 68 years.

John Mason junior had seen the need for a general carrying service. Though at first he had only a pony and cart he soon expanded the small business by offering to carry anything anywhere. The firm's early records show that a wide variety of goods were carried including laundry to and from the large houses of the wealthy merchants living in the residential districts of Wavertree and Woolton. One early contract was to carry laundry for the Liverpool School for the Blind between its Wavertree and its Liverpool premises - a contract held until 1958 when the city establishment closed.

John Mason married Mary Hannah Baker in 1897. From then on she assisted her husband with the clerical and book-keeping work. She would later continue to do so for her sons in their turn.

Before long more vehicles and heavier horses were acquired. Furniture vans were built to John Mason's requirements. From the firm's base a terraced house, at 85, High Street, the Mason family home, the first long distance removals were undertaken in 1900 using horse-drawn vehicles.

***Above:** Where it all began, Mrs Mary Mason outside her home in 85 High Street, Wavertree, in 1900. **Below left:** John Mason with one of his first horse and carts. **Below:** The original Mason family.*

Early customers included the Anglo American Oil Company, which would eventually become Esso, the Cheshire Lines Railway Company, and the English Margarine Works.

When work started on the Liverpool Anglican Cathedral in 1904, the very-aptly named John Mason carried much of the carved stonework for the building contractor, Morrisons Ltd.

The firm's activities soon extended not only to Liverpool but also to Manchester, many parts of Lancashire, Cheshire, and North Wales using horse-drawn vehicles. Longer distances, those over 50 miles, were covered by rail.

Liverpool was growing, and as new districts were being developed, contracts were obtained from the City Corporation to carry material for the new roads being constructed. John Mason was a man of great energy and enterprise and never afraid of hard work - if necessary round the clock.

John Mason had a great passion for horses: his only hobby was buying and selling them for himself and for others. His judgement was so respected that he bought and sold horses for a number of the principal dock contractors, and even Lord Sefton entrusted him with commissions to buy horses on his behalf. John would regularly spend a day each month at the Craven Arms Horse Repository; he was also keen on entering his horses in agricultural shows, where his horses won many prizes.

By the outbreak of the First World War in 1914 John Mason had built up a thriving firm engaged in coal retailing, general haulage and household removals. Although the shortage of horses during the war would restrict business, John's astuteness ensured that the business did not falter. In 1917 the business moved to 127, High Street, Wavertree, gaining more space for warehousing and stabling for the firm's horses.

Leslie Mason, John and Mary's eldest son born in 1904, entered the business in his early teens; he would play a full part in the firm for almost fifty years. Leslie had shown an early interest from childhood: at the age of only 12 he was already helping by driving a pony and wagon like his father before him. By the age of 16 Leslie was driving a team of horses, helping to overcome the wartime manpower shortage and learning the business from a practical point of view.

When the firm's first motor vehicle, an Albion, was acquired in 1921 it had solid tyres and a chain drive. Although more motor vehicles would be steadily added to the fleet, horse transport would still be the main form of transport for some time, and horses continued to be bought for many years. It would not be until almost the outbreak of the Second World War that all horse-drawn vehicles would be wholly replaced by motor vans, platform vehicles and lift vans.

Top left: *John Mason driving one of his first horse-drawn vans.* ***Left:*** *One of the first motor vehicles to be purchased - French manufactured Aries.* ***Above:*** *Leslie Mason.* ***Below:*** *One of the first Albion's, purchased in the early 1920s.*

In the meantime, with the increasing help of Leslie Mason, the business developed. Its reputation for good workmanship and the personal attention and courtesy of its employees became ever more widely known.

The first lift vans for rail had been bought in 1926 and overseas agents were appointed to look after the firm's interests abroad. In 1938, a year before the outbreak of the Second World War, John Mason's second son, Stanley, joined the family firm. Born in 1921, Stanley would play a major role in developing the company, but his practical training involving driving and packing was interrupted in 1941 by being called up to serve in the Merchant Navy for the duration of the war.

Just as in the First World War the demand for house moves was much reduced, though contracts gained from the Government helped keep the business going despite both a manpower shortage and petrol rationing.

The Second World War, which brought to an end the era of the horse-drawn vehicle, saw the firm's motorised vehicles being utilised for war service. One of the many interesting jobs undertaken was transporting the Royal Liverpool Philharmonic Orchestra's instruments around the country, enabling it to continue to give regular performances. The orchestra gave many concerts to troops and civilians during the war years. Mason's driver, Bill Clarke, was never late for a concert even though he had to contend with all the hazards of the blackout and enemy bombing.

During those years Masons also did vital work evacuating schools, institutions, government departments, commercial and industrial concerns and homes. Munitions and other war equipment were carried, whilst to meet the call for decentralisation extra warehouses were acquired on the outskirts of the city and at Penmaenmawr, in North Wales, for furniture storage. Each evening during the intense bombing of Liverpool the Mason team played its part with Mason vehicles reporting for duty at Civil Defence and Fire Posts.

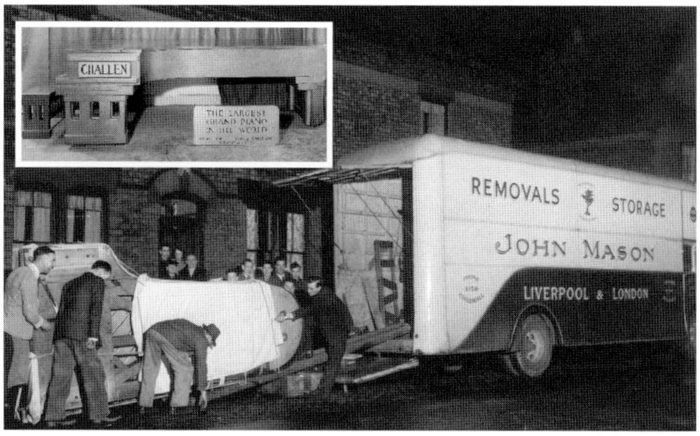

The war's end in 1945 brought with it the enormous problems of rebuilding after the destruction of the blitz. Industry and commerce had to be reorganised to meet the needs of the post-war world. The Mason brothers, with hard work and foresight, made great progress. Large office removals were undertaken, and a considerable contribution made to the transport services required by the vast rebuilding programme which would take place.

Top left: *Mason's first pneumatic tyred vehicle. A forerunner of the modern fleet.* ***Left:*** *International Removal circa 1930s.* ***Bottom left:*** *This vehicle was contracted to the Royal Liverpool Philharmonic Orchestra's to transport instruments around the country.* ***Above:*** *Moving the largest piano in the world (inset) in 1956.* ***Below:*** *In the 1950s John Mason were responsible for shipping this car belonging to Queen Elizabeth II.*

A daily removal service to Ireland using the Preston/Larne roll-on roll-off ferry began in 1955. Combined with the daily Liverpool/London service this offered the fastest route available from the capital to Ireland. Mason's would be one of the first removal firms to use the ferry service from Preston, and at the time be the only firm in the north west offering an almost daily service to Ireland of articulated trailer vans. The service offered considerable savings in packing and handling costs, since loading on and off the ferry by crane was no longer needed.

Weeks of pre-planning were sometimes necessary for the removals of private and government offices to ensure the minimum disruption of office routine, and several had to be undertaken at weekends. Hundreds of tons of files, papers and office equipment were involved in one of the largest moves in which the Inland Revenue, Ministry of Food and other Ministerial offices were transferred from Llandudno to London.

A daily removal service from Liverpool to London was started in 1948; London depot facilities would be eventually acquired from FL Pettman Ltd to facilitate distribution in the London area and arrange return loads. In 1950, the company became one of the founder members of FIDI - the world-wide Federation of International Furniture Removers.

John Mason junior, who had retired at the end of the war, died in 1953. His sons Leslie and Stanley were by then joint Managing Directors. By 1948 the business had grown to such an extent that the private limited company of John Mason (Wavertree) Ltd had been formed with John and Mary Mason, with sons Leslie and Stanley, as its directors.

To ensure reliability all vehicles had always to be kept in first class condition so that delivery promises could be honoured. Now the fleet and equipment would be kept constantly up to date by the purchase of new vehicles. Steady expansion of Mason's service was made to cover the whole of the United Kingdom.

To help provide a more local service in Cheshire in 1955 Leslie and Stanley became directors of B Dudley & Sons Ltd - Removers of Bebington, a firm established in 1869. Both companies worked in close association. In 1959 Dudley's would be taken over completely by Masons.

Top left and above: *The roll-on roll-off ferry service from Preston to Larne, Mason's were one of the first companies to use this service with the Empire Cedric Vessel, picture above.* ***Bottom left:*** *Stanley Mason.* ***Top right:*** *A John Mason container being loaded.* ***Below:*** *Delivering a grand piano to the QEII.*

By the end of the 1950s Masons, in association with four reputable South of England firms, had also established a network of distribution routes serving the Midlands, the South West, the South East and the South of England as well as many parts of Wales, Lancashire and Yorkshire.

A new 16,000 sq. ft warehouse was opened in Wavertree in 1959, built to the company's specifications and specially designed and constructed to store customers' effects with the highest possible degree of safety. By 1962 the continued growth of the company resulted in the purchase of a 36,000 sq. ft warehouse in Kirby.

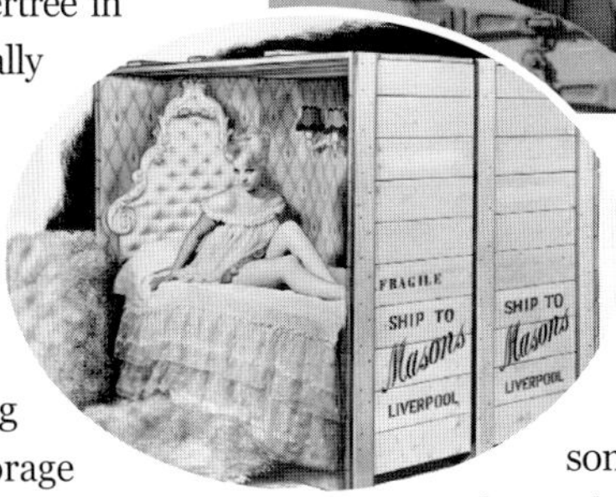

The company now launched into the antique shipping business, which required large consolidation and storage facilities. By 1967 a further 2,000 sq. ft warehouse was acquired bringing the company's total Merseyside facilities to 72,000 sq ft.

Stanley Mason was elected President of the Overseas Division of the British Association of Removers in 1965. Six years later, however, 1971 began with Leslie Mason's death. Stanley's wife, Jean, now joined her husband as a director: their eldest son Paul entered the business in 1972.

The company joined 'Eurovan', a consortium of around 180 mainly privately-owned world wide removal companies in 1974. By 1977 a record volume of antique shipping was recorded - some 250 ISO containers were packed and despatched from the company's warehouses. By 1982 that success was consolidated with a record year for inter-continental removals: over 400 containers were exported, winning the company the Eurovan 'Biggest Booker' of the year award.

Top left: *Household removals in the 1950s.* ***Left:*** *Jean Mason and son, Paul.* ***Top right:*** *John Mason advertising of the 1960s.* ***Above inset:*** *Mason's won first prize in an FIDI photography competition in the section entitled "A Most Beautiful Removal".* ***Below:*** *Trade Co-operation in 1963. John Mason undertook a move for Imperial Chemical Industries (ICI). The ICI offices were being moved from the Royal Liver Buildings, Liverpool to Runcorn. The move was a joint effort between John Mason, Colemans Ltd and Pickfords. The vehicles are seen here in Brunswick Street ready for the call.*

Stanley Mason died suddenly whilst on holiday, in April 1983. His son Paul Mason now joined his mother Jean as a director of the company ably helped by Cris O'Hara, whom Stanley had earlier hired to run the office, and by newly recruited Bob Clarke who had trained with Pickfords.

Exactly a century of successful trading had been achieved, not only through the hard work of the directors but very much because the company had always enjoyed a loyal and hard working staff. Their contribution above all else has played the central role in the growth and development of the business. It was in that spirit that in 1984 the firm entered its second century.

In 1989 all the company's local activities were transferred to 35, Wilson Road, Huyton, whilst a new warehouse and offices were opened in Croydon.

Sadly, Paul Mason passed away in 2009. His wife Vivien then became a Director. The fifth generation of the family, Caroline and Simon Mason, joined the business in the same year. Caroline graduated from the University of Leeds with a degree in Business Management and Spanish and Simon from the University of Manchester, achieving a First Class degree in International Business. Since joining the company, both Caroline and Simon have embarked on an extensive training programme within the industry: Simon completed most of his training in the

USA, and Caroline learned about the business in both Liverpool and London.

Today, international, commercial and household moves and storage remain at the core of the firm's business. Mason's currently facilitates over 8,000 removals each year across the globe. From a single horse and cart and undertaking only local work, John Mason International Ltd has grown into a major player on the world stage. But despite its growth the firm retains the virtues of a family firm: flexibility, a genuine appreciation of its employees, and an unswerving commitment to meeting its clients' needs.

Top left: *Cris O'Hara and Bob Clarke.* ***Top right:*** *John Mason's International House, Huyton Business Park, premises.* ***Centre :*** *John Mason International's 130th anniversary cake.* ***Below:*** *Staff and management celebrating the company's 130th anniversary in 2014. The fifth generation of the family, Caroline and Simon Mason can be seen front left.*

Merchant Taylors' School

The Best Education for Life

MERCHANT TAYLORS' SCHOOLS

For Boys and Girls aged 4 to 18 years

The desire to get a good education is an ancient and honourable one. Education has always been the key to a successful life. Because of that fact those who have found success in life almost invariably look back to 'the happiest days of their lives' and give due credit to the academic institutions which helped forge their characters.

For four centuries Merseyside folk have been fortunate in being able to obtain an excellent education locally, ever since the reign of James I.

Merchant Taylors' are a famous family of Schools for boys and girls aged 4-18 years. With a consistent 100% pass rate at A Level and 80% of all grades at A* to B, their academic reputation is second to none in the area.

This famous schools in Crosby were founded as a grammar school for boys by John Harrison in 1620, the year in which the Pilgrim Fathers first settled in New England. Well known former pupils include Robert Runcie, Archbishop of Canterbury from 1980 to 1991, and the novelist Dame Beryl Bainbridge. Amongst the staff, playwright Terence Rattigan taught Classics at the Boys' school before writing the famous work 'The Winslow Boy'.

Since its founding the original school has become four schools: a combined co-educational prep and junior girls' school known as Merchant Taylors' Primary School, Stanfield (MTPS), a boys' junior school, and two senior schools situated on separate sites - one each for boys and girls.

The schools today are led by the Chair of Governors, Professor Peter Batey, appointed in 2011. Headmaster, David Cook, of the Boys' School joined in September 2005 and Louise Robinson, Headmistress of the Girls' School was appointed in 2006. The Junior Schools are headed up by Mrs Janet Thomas looking after the Junior Boys' School and Miss Julie Yardley in charge of MTPS. Single sex education is at the core of the schools, although boys and girls are taught in mixed classes up to Year 3.

The schools' founder, John Harrison, was a member of the Merchant Taylors' Company in London where he owned considerable amounts of land, as well as in Yorkshire, Berkshire and Essex.

Top left: *The school crest.* ***Above left:*** *The old school, which was built in 1620 to house 60 boys, is still in use today as part of the girls' school library.* ***Left:*** *The whole school pictured in 1871 outside the old school house.* ***Above:*** *Heads of Merchant Taylors' Schools, L-R: David Cook, Louise Robinson, Julie Yardley and Janet Thomas.*

On his death John Harrison left enormous assets, part of which was bequeathed to the Merchant Taylors' Company to act as Trustees for his school in Crosby, a role they would retain until 1910.

The first Headmaster was the Revd John Kidde, followed (amongst others) by men still very much part of the School life who give their names to Houses or buildings, such as John Stevens, John Waring, Wilfred Troutbeck, Canon Samuel Armour, Thomas York, and Mark Luft.

The original building still stands in Crosby, as part of Merchant Taylors' Girls' School (MTGS) but is hidden from view by the newer buildings on Liverpool Road.

The 'Guild and Fraternity of St. John the Baptist, time out of mind called tailors and linen armourers of London' had been in existence since at least in 1300 when it was recorded that 'they chose Henry de Ryall to be their pilgrim'. Letters Patent of Edward III issued in 1327 record Royal acceptance of the Guild in its first Charter.

One legacy of those far-off days is the commonly used phrase 'all at sixes and sevens' meaning, 'all confused', or 'in disagreement'. The expression stems from the days when the Merchant Taylors' Company and the Merchant Skinners' Company were unable to agree amongst themselves as to which of the two ancient companies was the more senior – in 1484 Richard III was seeking to put his Guilds into ranking order; the Lord Mayor of London, one Billesden's, wise Solomon-like solution to the disagreement was that one year the Taylors' were ranked sixth, with the Skinners seventh, and vice versa the following year. This became known as the principle of 'sixes and sevens'. Of course this hardly resolved the question, but it provided a fitting solution to the disagreement!

Between 1512 and 1620 there had already been five schools and colleges established by Merchant Taylors' Company in England and Ireland – and now there was about to be a sixth.

John Harrison's father came from Great Crosby, and for several years before his death, John had it in mind to build and endow a free grammar school in his father's home village - for teaching, educating and instructing children and youth in the grammar and rules of learning forever.

The 1620s building is one of the oldest buildings still in use in Sefton. In 2009 a new front entrance to the Girls' School was built. It provides a modern open frontage to the School. The Vitreum, as it is known, also contains an art gallery in the upper level which has seen many well known local artists present their exhibitions. The Patron of the Vitreum is Ben Johnson.

Top left and above: *Early 20th century classrooms.* ***Left:*** *An informal staff photograph of some members taken between 1904 and 1910. From bottom left, clockwise: Miss Mackenzie, Miss Mason, Miss Malpas, Miss Birchall, Mrs Burrows and Miss Mallaker.*

Meanwhile, during Canon Armour's headship (1863-1903), the School had the chance to expand and develop. It grew into an important day school, standing on an equal footing with the best ancient public schools in the country.

The Boys' School moved to an imposing new building in 1878. Since then this has been a famous landmark in Crosby, on the Liverpool to Southport road. It is a fine example of Victorian architecture, with an imposing clock tower.

Merchant Taylors' Girls' School was founded in 1888, having inherited the buildings from the boys' school that had moved 'up the road' in 1878. The then governing body was dilatory in providing for the 'new' school and it was only due to the insistence of James Fenning, the Master of the Worshipful Company of Merchant Taylors, that the girls' school was started. At the School's opening the female staff were all graduates, a fact that is very impressive considering that at the time only four universities were granting degrees to women! In June 1888 twelve pupils attended the school, by the 1920s this figure had grown to 300 and now has more than doubled to around 600.

Above left: *Merchant Taylors' Girls' School, Crosby, featuring a new front entrance.* ***Above:*** *The Tennis Team, 1926. Pictured from left to right, back row: Peggy Grant, Ethel Hiller-Hughes, Doris Gerrard, front row: Joan Williams (Vice Captain) Hazel Thornton (Captain) and Lillian Kenworthy.* ***Below:*** *A famous landmark in Crosby, the Victorian School was opened in 1878 by the Countess of Derby.*

The continuing increase in pupil numbers enabled the purchase in 1911 of the adjoining house, 'The Mulberries', which doubled the existing space and still adds to the charm of the school.

The jewel of the buildings, the now Grade II listed 1620s building (currently housing the library), has always dominated the surrounding area and new buildings. Two generous donations from a former headmistress ensured further development of facilities forming the basis of the current network of buildings.

The early girls' curriculum was based on a limited version of the boys', with little Mathematics or Latin - in case it taxed the female brain - and plenty of 'feminine' subjects such as singing and needlework to placate worries of producing only 'blue stocking' and thus almost guaranteed spinsterhood. The curriculum today, offering so much opportunity and variety, would have been hugely envied by the early girls.

Celebrating the centenary for the girls' in 1988 the school played host to Prince Andrew and Sarah Duchess of York. At this time the Centenary Hall was built and new facilities developed for science, modern languages and home economics.

Academically Merchant Taylors' Schools have been consistently placed amongst the top schools in the North-West – they have also achieved outstanding sporting success in all disciplines. Though MTS has always had an excellent academic tradition, its pupils are now able to sample numerous extra-curricular activities.

As for younger students, MTPS Stanfield is the Merchant Taylors' mixed prep school and also the junior school for girls. It is located on its own site between the Boys' and Girls' Senior schools sites. It has been in this current position since 1946, and has during recent years seen major redevelopment with a new building. Pupils are able to use the senior schools' facilities such as the sports centre and swimming pool situated at the Boys' school.

Following the expansion of the Prep to two-form entry, in early 1998 Alan Hansen, former Liverpool football star (whose son started in the Preparatory department at MTS in 1988), opened the new classroom block and enlarged hall for the Prep - which was at the same time re-named as the Merchant Taylors' Junior Boys' School.

Throughout the twentieth century, the School has moved with the times - making the successful transition from Public School to Direct Grant, and in due course, to Independent status. The abolition of the Government Assisted Places Scheme in 2002, which supported over 30% of the Schools' intake, was replaced by the introduction of an Assisted Places Scheme fully funded by the Schools, mainly through generous donations from alumni into the Schools' Bursary Fund.

The Girls' and Boys' Schools' have faced up to the future of competitive education, and succeeded in consistently maintaining some of the best academic results in the North West. During previous inspections the Schools have been commended with a glowing report as being outstanding in its many achievements, not just academically, but also in their many extra-curricular activities: music, drama, sport, Combined Cadet Force, and through the many societies which give pupils a chance to experience far more of life than just that inside the classroom.

Top left: *Prince Andrew and Sarah Duchess of York's celebratory visit to the school in 1988.* ***Above:*** *Merchant Taylors' Head Boys and Head Girls, 2014/15.* ***Below:*** *Reception pupils from MTPS, Stanfield.*

As the Merchant Taylors' Company's ancient Latin motto in the school crest says 'Concordia parvae res crescunt' - 'small things grow in harmony' - so the Schools' whole ethos is one in which a warm, and friendly atmosphere fosters the best which pupils have to offer, developing them to their full potential, and preparing them for the challenges of the modern world beyond. Today the modern schools' motto however is in English - 'The Best Education for Life' - for most that personal preparation includes participation in such challenging sports and other extra-curricular activities as drama, music, rowing, sailing and the Combined Cadet Force where they have the opportunity of attending a variety of camps and courses, both in Great Britain and overseas. Both boys and girls are encouraged to take part in the Duke of Edinburgh Award Scheme, and many achieve success in Bronze, Silver and Gold awards.

The schools also play an active role in the local community; they carry out many fundraising activities for local charities such as Alder Hey and the NSPCC.

In September 2011 Merchant Taylors' Schools saw the opening of a new £5.5 million facility called the Ian Robinson Sports Centre. Located at the Boys' School site on Liverpool Road, this ambitious development designed by Buttress Fuller Alsop Williams Architects, is benefiting all pupils from the family of Merchant Taylors' Schools, and includes a dance studio, fitness suite and a large indoor facility equipped to provide state-of-the-art facilities for rugby training, football, hockey, tennis, badminton and many other sports.

Alongside this new period of development for the Schools a new two-year campaign called Sporting Start was launched in 2010, marking the first milestone in a new ongoing period of fundraising. Between 2002 and 2008 the Schools successfully raised over £1 million to support the ongoing Bursary Fund. Following on from this the Governors set the objective of raising a further £1 million to secure that fund, as well as £1 million to invest in a number of capital build developments being made at the Schools over the current decade when the Schools celebrate their 400th Anniversary in 2020.

The title 'Sporting Start' refers to the opportunities the Bursary Fund provides, by giving a child a sporting start in life.

Top left: *Year 1 girls from Merchant Taylors' Girls Junior School - Stanfield pose for a photograph for the 1953 prospectus brochure.* ***Left:*** *Pupils from the Junior Boys' School.* ***Above:*** *Sport is a big part of life at Merchant Taylors' - pictured are the U16 Hockey County Champions.* ***Above right:*** *Young biathletes from the Junior Girls' School.*

In 2015 Mrs Abila Pointing MBE DL, the High Sheriff of Merseyside, officially opened a multi-million pound redevelopment at Merchant Taylors' Primary School, Stanfield, providing new facilities for 360 students. The two year project undertaken by Eric Wright Construction was completed in December 2014 and was the second major build project at Merchant Taylors' Schools, in the previous five years. It is part of an overall 10 year development strategy.

The launch was marked by an official steel signing ceremony in 2013 by Liverpool Captain Steven Gerrard.

Miss Julie Yardley, Head of Merchant Taylors' Primary School, Stanfield said "I am delighted with this superb new build. The much needed redevelopment incorporates a new large hall and kitchens, several classrooms, resource rooms, practice rooms and a dedicated library as well as a fully equipped medical room and other bespoke rooms for specialist teaching of IT, art, music and drama. The staff, pupils and parents are absolutely thrilled with the new facilities."

For nearly four centuries MTS has been the best academic and all round independent school in the North West: it is set fair to continue to be so for the next 400 years.

Top left:*The School carries a long tradition of excellence in Rugby.* ***Left and below:*** *Mrs Abila Pointing MBE DL, the High Sheriff of Merseyside, officially opens the redeveloped Merchant Taylors' Primary School, Stanfield, pictured below.* ***Above:*** *A family of Schools.*

Rathbone Brothers Plc

Investing in Liverpool since 1742

Today, the Liverpool-based company Rathbone Brothers Plc, is through its subsidiaries, one of the UK's leading providers of investment management services for private clients, charities and professional advisers. With £27.2 billion of funds under management it has over 39,000 clients.

When it was established, however, the original business was not that of an investment manager but a merchant.

The first record of the company is from 1742 and William Rathbone II. In his leather-bound Day Book of that year, William's extensive work as a timber merchant is recorded. Before founding his own business William had moved from Gawsworth to Liverpool in 1725 to work as a sawyer.

William seized every opportunity and it was not long before his timber and ship building firm was thriving. The business was run from premises at Duke and Hanover Streets and provided goods to a variety of clients including cabinet makers, clock-makers, ship owners and builders in places such as Wallasey, Sefton and Wavertree. From eight to twelve men were employed at the yard including William's son. William III, who joined the firm in 1745.

-

Rathbones' founder died in 1746. However, the extensive links he made with his Quaker friends stood the firm in good stead, amongst then Elizabeth Fry and Richard Reynolds the philanthropists, and the banking families Gurney and Tuke: all later became business associates.

William III introduced a merchanting business which flourished to become world-wide. Timber was purchased for the yard from a network of agents in Amsterdam, Danzig, Barbados and Boston and, to fill empty cargo space, other goods such as tallow, iron bars, wheat, sugar, salt, coffee, lead, tobacco, leather and ginger were sold with 2.5 per cent commission plus shipping charges. Despite his ambitious nature William refused to make any profit out of the growing slave trade.

By 1768, the firm had added several warehouses and buildings to its premises and also owned several ships. In 1789, William extended the premises again but this time the development caused a dispute with the Duke of Bridgewater who alleged that his dock had been damaged during the work. The dispute was not settled until 1792! Nevertheless, on his death in 1789 William III left a highly successful business to his son William IV who had already been helping to run the firm for many years. Unlike his father and grandfather, William IV found narrow Quaker doctrines untenable, and after publishing 'A Narrative of Events that have lately taken place in Ireland among the Society called Quakers' he was formally disunited from the Society.

William's liberal and reforming spirit also led him to work for the abolition of the slave trade, and in turn to concentrate on trading activities with North America.

Above: *William Rathbone III, 1726-1789.* ***Below:*** *A drawing of the port of Liverpool in 1728 by Samuel and Nathaniel Buck.*

By the 1800s, the Rathbone business had turned its concentration solely to merchanting and to 25, 100-300 ton ships with names such as Diana, Kitty, Active and Favorite, sailing to America and Canada, importing American pitch, tar, turpentine, 'new mess' in pork barrels and half barrels, barrel staves and rice.

It was also at this time that American cotton first made an appearance. Indeed, although not true, Rathbones gained a reputation for being the first firm to import American cotton because the Custom House, which did not know cotton was grown in America, notoriously seized the firm's first importation.

In order to cope with the increased workload William IV had taken on a partner in 1790, his sister's husband, Robert Benson, and the firm became known as Rathbone & Benson Merchants. In 1795, another partner, James Cropper, was taken on. However, a year later, due to ill health, both partners left and were replaced by William Hughes and William McMurdo Duncan who bought £2,000 worth of shares each from Robert Benson. Together in 1801, William IV and William McMurdo Duncan served on the founding committee of the Liverpool American Chamber of Commerce. In contrast, William Hughes did not have such a good relationship with the partners and left the firm ill 1809. Sadly, this was also the year of William IV's death.

However, he left a prosperous business and a large fortune to his sons William V and Richard. The old partnership of Rathbone, Hughes and Duncan was automatically dissolved, but still William Hughes tried to put obstacles in the way of William V and Richard joining the firm. In the end, Hughes and Duncan continued to trade in the firm's old style and the brothers set up on their own account as commission merchants. Fortunately, the first goods arrival after these events was consigned to the brothers' firm rather than to Hughes and Duncan and the Rathbones did not look back.

In 1814, Adam Hodgson joined the business which became Rathbone Hodgson and Co until 1824 when it changed again to Rathbone Bros and Co, the name it retained. Two years before this Rathbones had helped in establishing Whittaker, Whitehead amd Co. William V and Richard's younger brother Theodore became a partner in this leading brokerage firm and consequently Rathbones used the firm for the cotton commission work which had become the mainstay of their business.

In 1835, Richard Rathbone retired and was replaced by Edward Dearman. Under his guidance Rathbones was moved up town, away from the river to new premises in Castle Street.

Top: *An engraving of Ironbridge George, Coalbrookdale, by James Fittler, published in 1788. The Rathbones family remained trustees and major shareholders in the Bridge until 1950.* ***Above left:*** *William Rathbone IV, 1757-1809, painted by J Allen.* ***Right:*** *The statue of William Rathbone V in Sefton Park.*

Although the period of the 1820s to the 1840s was a time of decline for the cotton consignment business which was being strangled by stringent regulations, Rathbones managed to maintain its success. The firm reached a landmark in its history when it became involved in the inauguration of the first regular line of ships sailing to New York. Further work followed and it was not long before Rathbones also ran a regular line of packets to Philadelphia.

The year 1842 was also an important one for Rathbones as William V's two eldest sons, William VI and Samuel joined the firm which at the time had a capital of £40,000. William VI joined as a partner whilst Samuel was not made partner until 1847. Along with Thomas K Twist, Samuel and William VI established Rathbone Houses at Canton and Shanghai from where they sold British-manufactured goods in China and bought tea and silk for export to Britain and later to America. This side of the business was highly profitable. However, due to practical and moral problems Canton House was closed in 1850, closely followed by the one in Shanghai.

From then on Rathbones' trading interests in China were run using other firms.

Throughout the 1840s Rathbones' American trade consisted mainly of importing cotton and breadstuffs to the UK, and mainly exporting tea from China and coffee from Brazil to America.

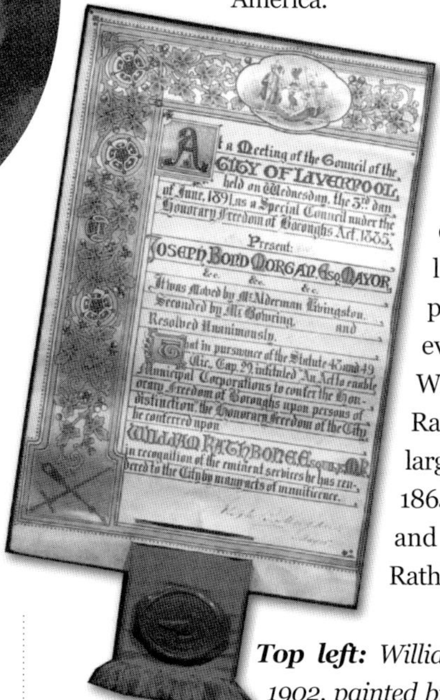

At a Meeting of the Council of the City of Liverpool, held on Wednesday, the 3rd day of June, 1891, as a Special Council under the "Honorary Freedom of Boroughs Act, 1885."
Present:
Joseph Bond Morgan Esq. Mayor
&c. &c. &c.
It was Moved by Mr Alderman Livingston, Seconded by Mr Gowring, and Resolved Unanimously.
That in pursuance of the Statute 48 and 49 Vic., Cap. 29 intituled "An Act to enable Municipal Corporations to confer the Honorary Freedom of Boroughs upon persons of distinction" the Honorary Freedom of the City be conferred upon
William Rathbone Esq. M.P.
in recognition of the eminent services he has rendered to the City by many acts of munificence.

By 1851, however, trade had increased to such an extent that an agency in New York was established. Henry Gair established the agency, and later, in 1854, became a partner. His position was eventually taken over by William Lidderdale who saw Rathbones become one of the largest China tea importers. In 1864, he too was made a partner and subsequently established Rathbones' London House.

Top left: *William Rathbone VI, MP, 1819-1902, painted by Sir William Richmond RA.* ***Above:*** *The Honorary Freedom of Liverpool, granted to William Rathbone VI on June 3, 1891.* ***Left:*** *Samuel Greg Rathbone, who joined the family firm in 1842.* ***Below:*** *The Rathbone ship 'Scawfell', which made several record voyages between the Far East and England in the mid-1800s.*

By the 1860s, sail was starting to be replaced by steam and Rathbones joined with Lamport and Holt to build four steamers. In 1864, the fleet of the Liverpool Brazil and River Plate Steamship Navigation Company was formed in which Rathbones held the controlling share. The other major development at this time was Rathbones' collaboration with Ross T Smythe in the corn trade.

William Rathbone VI, who after witnessing the care his dying wife required, took it upon himself to campaign for the provision of nursing to the poor. Working alongside Florence Nightingale, he helped set up the Liverpool Training School and Home for Nurses in 1862. His work also included assisting the formation of the University of Liverpool, to which the family left a number of properties.

Throughout the 1880s the representatives from Smythe and Rathbones became directors in North Shore Rice and Flour Mills.

In 1889 Hugh Rathbone became the last working partner in the business when William VI retired. It was also in that year that the firm's shipping operations came to an end when the Starline steamers were sold to Harrisons of Liverpool.

Later in the 19th century, two ladies were born into the family, who would further their family's good work. Eleanor Rathbone, the daughter of William Rathbone VI, was one of the first female magistrates. In 1929, she became an independent MP, campaigning for social housing reform, women's right to vote and family allowances. Eleanor's cousin, Elfrida Rathbone, upheld the right for all children to be educated; she also set up one of the earliest centres for women with mental and physical disabilities.

Meanwhile, the 1890s were years of crisis for Rathbones. There was a shortage of merchanting talent in the Rathbone family to replace the previous generation. William VI's son, William Gair VIII, was a partner in the London House but, after his brother Thomas Ashton's early death, there was no one to take over the Liverpool side of the business. Eventually, Arthur Rudford was appointed this role, but in 1898 the existing partnership was dissolved, the London House was closed and the Liverpool business was re-established on a reduced scale with supervision from the partners of Ross T Smythe. Unfortunately, the firm's fortunes did not increase. There were losses in the wheat and wool operations and by the 1900s the merchanting business was a shadow of its former self. 1902 and 1903 saw the deaths of William VI and Samuel respectively. Francis 'Frank' Warre Rathbone now became partner.

Arthur Radford and Robert Rathbone were in charge of the Liverpool office and were joined briefly by William VIII who sadly, proved unsuitable for partnership.

Top left: *William Gair Rathbone (VII), William Rathbone (VIII) and William Rathbone (VI) pictured in 1895. All three were associated with Rathbone Bros, over the years 1842-1914.* ***Left:*** *Francis Warre Rathbone who joined the firm in 1902 and remained a partner until his death in 1939.* ***Below:*** *Eleanor Florence Rathbone, MP, daughter of William Rathbone VI, who was concerned with many campaigns for social and political reform.*

By 1912 Arthur and Robert had retired and the restructuring of the firm was completed with a move to modern premises in the Royal Liver Building under Frank's capable leadership. An investment trust started in 1911 brought the business considerable profits and it was this, combined with the dedication of Vere Cotton, who became a partner in 1919, that kept the firm afloat during the First World War.

During the inter-war years, in 1934, Frank's son, Bertram Lyle (Larry) Rathbone, joined the firm and five years later, on his father's death, was made partner. The advent of the Second World War saw Larry joining the army and leaving Vere in sole charge of the Liverpool office which was now requisitioned.

New premises were found at Brunswick Street, but this building and all the records in it were destroyed by a bomb in 1941. Rathbones moved again, this time to Castle Street.

When Larry rejoined the firm after the war time was spent developing Rathbones' client base. Post-war growth included the addition of a total of 500 accounts and the enlargement of the range of private clients. In 1949, Rathbones also became involved with the Albany Investment Trust, taking over the administration of the company.

Throughout the 1960s Rathbones established links with the merchant banker A Keyser and Co and formed a joint company Keyser Ullman Rathbone Ltd which operated for ten years. Vere retired and was succeeded by Larry, Sebastian Rathbone and John Leigh.

Above: *The retirement party for Vere Cotton (standing 6th from the right) in 1960. Larry Rathbone, his successor and senior partner is to Vere's right. Sebastian Rathbone is on the extreme left.* ***Left:*** *John Leigh, Roy Morris, Sebastian Rathbone, Anthony Nottingham and Anthony Furse, partners of Rathbone Bros. & Co. in the late 1980s.* ***Below:*** *Rathbones Cowes Week boat, 2006.*

The decade was one of success, and as a result Rathbones gained a good reputation for giving advice on taxation.

In 1971, Comprehensive Financial services (later Rathbone Bros plc) was incorporated and this was followed by Larry's retirement from senior partnership in 1979. Sebastian took his place and was joined by a string of new partners including Anthony Furse in 1972, Roy Morris in 1983 and Anthony Nottingham in 1987.

By 1984, Rathbones had become so successful that its shares were quoted on the London Stock Exchange.

The year 1988 was a significant one in the company's history. The Rathbone Group expanded through an amalgamation of the investment management and banking business in Liverpool with the international trust and company management and investment management business in London.

The years 1995, 1996 and 1998 were marked by further growth. Several firms were acquired including Laurence Keen and Neilson Cobbold, both of them investment management companies in Scotland, and a trust business in Jersey.

Since the millennium Rathbones has opened offices in Winchester, Birmingham, Aberdeen, Edinburgh, Newcastle and Lymington to add to those in Cambridge, Exeter, Kendal and Bristol. The London office has relocated to 1 Curzon Street. A new office in Glasgow will be the latest addition, due to open in 2015.

Roy Morris retired as Chief executive in 2004 to be replaced by Andy Pomfret, who would in turn be succeeded by Philip Howell in 2014. The current Chaiman is Mark Nicholls who was appointed on 11 May, 2011.

Today, this multiple-award winning business is looking forward with confidence to growth in the 21st century, just as much as its founder William Rathbone II did back in 1742.

Top left and top right: *Rathbones' London office at 1 Curzon Street.* ***Left:*** *Rathbones' Pier Head, Liverpool, office.* ***Above:*** *Philip Howell, Chief Executive.* ***Right:*** *Mark Nicholls, Chairman.*

EG Everton Glass

A Tale of Tiles

Our homes may be our castles but we certainly don't want them to look like draughty old ruins. For decades we seem to have been obsessed by home improvements; not least in the sort of tiles we expect to see in our kitchens and bathrooms.

Tiles have changed incredibly over what seems like a very short period of time. Today, if you look in the nation's kitchens and bathrooms there seems to be an incredible variety of ceramic tiles in use: plain and patterned, a whole rainbow of colours and an infinite variety of shapes and textures.

Of course, it wasn't always like that. Many readers' recollection of tiles in the home will be limited to those around the fireplace. The only place they were likely to see very large areas of tiles was in public buildings such as hospitals and museums where they tended to be of rather sober and uninspiring shades of brown and green. Yet, that is not the case today.

Inspired by endless television home improvement programmes, our homes are now almost invariably beautified by the addition of high quality ceramic tiles. And in Liverpool there is a good chance we bought them from EG Everton Glass.

Back in 1947, at the age of 41, Stanley Charles Richards a former glazier started the firm from premises at 19A Heyworth Street. From there he supplied glass, glazing and decorating products to the public and the trade. Eventually he would acquire two more shops in the area from where he would trade successfully for many years. During the mid-1960s, when Heyworth Street was being demolished, and whilst one side of the road was being pulled down, the firm acquired two shops on the opposite side, on the corner of Eastlake Street and Stansfield Road. By then Stanley's eldest son, Alan, had joined him and ran the decorating side of the business. A little later Stanley's youngest son, Stanley Jnr, came into the business and eventually worked in the glass, doors, and ceramic tiles section.

More moves would follow. The whole business was moved to 54-56 Townsend Lane in 1969, from where it continued to trade in exactly the same products. In 1972 the premises at 54-56 Townsend Lane were sold to Panorama Kitchens, and Everton Glass Works bought 60-64 Townsend Lane two doors further along.

When Pat Lewis, the founder's daughter, started working for the company in 1981, the firm bought 46-50 Townsend Lane and moved its glass and doors business there and later began selling ceramic tiles there too, leaving 60-64 for the decorating side of the business.

Company founder Stanley Richards died in 1983. The firm now passed to the next generation of the family.

Refurbishment was the order of the day in 1986 when 46-50 Townsend Lane was extensively altered and the tile side of the business, which by then was doing very well, was expanded. In 1991, because of increased business in ceramic tiles, the family acquired a 10,000 sq ft warehouse at 19A Belmont Road (clearly a lucky number, the second time it had turned up). Even that, however, was not enough. In 1997, after being unable to extend the warehouse in Belmont Road, and unable to get another property with a suitable warehouse in Liverpool, the firm now took the lease on a 6,000 sq ft warehouse in Bolton in order to cope with the expansion of the ceramic tile side of the business.

Following Alan's retirement his daughter Shirley would manage the wallpaper and decorating side of the business. Stanley's son Jonathan also joined the firm to manage the tile and door business. By 2001 the businesses in both Liverpool and Bolton were each subject to major refurbishment. This gave even more opportunities for customers to see all the stock that was available in Everton Glass Works showrooms. Three years later, in 2004, the firm bought a 40,000 sq ft warehouse in Bootle - Orrell Mount, in Hawthorne Road.

Top left, facing page: *Founder of the company, Stanley Charles Richards.* ***Bottom, facing page:*** *The Everton Glass Works premises on the corner of Eastlake Street and Heyworth Street in 1960s.* ***Above:*** *The firms former shop on the corner of Stansfield Road and Heyworth Street.* ***Below:*** *Townsend Lane Head Office in 2002.*

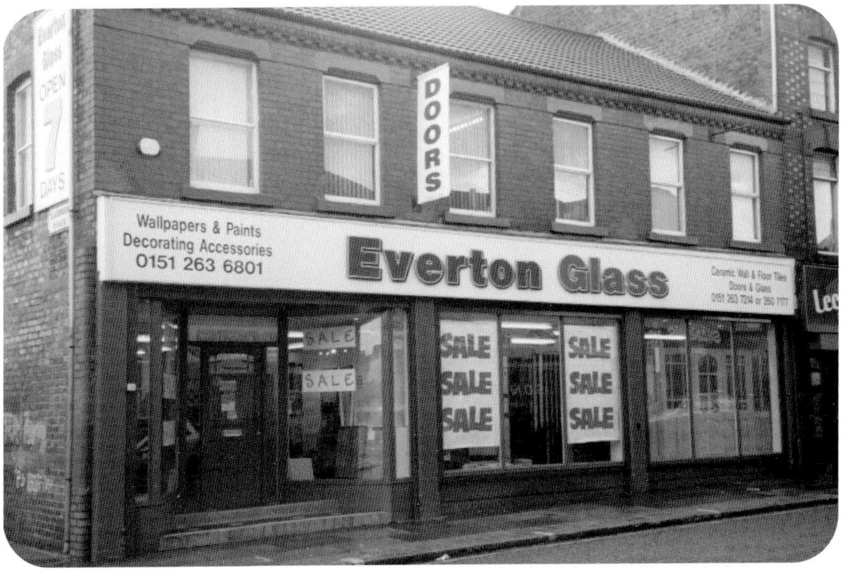

All stock was transferred to the Bootle warehouse. This made it possible to turn Belmont Road into just a tile showroom, making it at 10,000 sq ft one of, if not the largest, dedicated tile showroom in the North West. This helped with the increase of customers and also gave customers the opportunity to see displays of the tiles in situ.

In 2005 came the decision to close the showroom in Bolton in order to concentrate on the Liverpool branches. As more and more customers went to Belmont Road to view the tiles 46-50 Townsend Lane became less busy. To fit in with the modern way of displaying products it was decided to turn this shop into a dedicated door showroom of the highest calibre showcasing over 200 wooden doors on display as well as still offering a glass-cutting service.

In 2006 it was decided to make a small trade-showroom in the Bootle warehouse showing only tiles. Thus by 2006, 60-64 Townsend Lane was a wallpaper showroom, 46-50 Townsend Lane was a door showroom, 19A Belmont Road was a tile showroom and Orrell Mount, at Bootle, was a tile warehouse and trade counter. In subsequent years the Bootle trade counter became busier and busier and the showroom was extended a number of times, attracting a lot of new business from the north end of the city.

In 2010 the firm started to distribute tiles to a number of other tile showrooms in the North West. That side of the business has gone from strength to strength and is still growing today. This is due to us buying direct and in bulk from manufactures around the world. The following year it was decided to introduce bathroom furniture to the Bootle showroom as more and more customers wanted a 'one stop shop' for buying bathroom furniture and tiles. Yet, whilst one part of the business was growing, another was in decline. In 2012 due to a decline in the area and a drop in sales, it was with sadness that the decision was taken to close 46-50 and 60-64 Townsend Lane, where the company had thrived over the years.

Top left: *The company's Orrell Mount warehouse.* ***Above:*** *EG Everton Glass, 19A Belmont Road, Anfield.* ***Below:*** *EG Everton Glass' Bootle showroom.*

The door shop at 46-50 was closed first and relocated to Belmont Road; then in 2013 the wallpaper shop at 60-64 Townsend Lane was also moved. All wallpaper, paint, doors and bathroom furniture were in due course added to Belmont Road.

Meanwhile, at Bootle major work began on making a modern up to date showroom, incorporating tiles, bathroom furniture, doors, wallpaper and paints all under one roof, with the stock available to take away. At as the glass cutting service ceased the company rebranded itself, as EG Everton Glass. This was both to try and deflect people away from the fact that although it no longer supplied glass, whilst still wanting to keep the well-known Everton Glass name alive. Plus EG seemed a lot easier for people to remember

Today, the family firm has two 10,000 plus sq ft showrooms selling the latest designs in tiles, bathrooms, doors and wallpaper and paints. Stanley Richards has semi-retired from the company leaving his son, Jonathan Richards, to take overall control of the

company, with his cousin Shirley Richards still looking after the wallpaper side of things.

Everton Glass was always known as the place you could go and get a deal, which is still the case. What it has done over the years, however, is incorporate more higher-end products to cover the full spectrum of customers coming into the premises.

With two of the best interiors showrooms in the North West, the company offers something to fit everyone's budget, the one stop shop that has all they need. And as the firm's Radio ads say, 'EG, excellence guaranteed'.

Still a family run business offering good quality product at reasonable prices, Stanley Richards snr, the company founder, would have been astonished to see just how far the small business he established in Heyworth Street back in 1947 had managed to progress in a little over sixty years. He would probably be even more surprised to know just how obsessed the British have become with home improvements over that period. Thank goodness firms like EG Everton Glass exist in order to meet our apparently limitless appetites for such products. And thank goodness too that we have a wider choice of tiles today than the limited selection of utility white, institution brown and hospital green which were all that seemed to be on offer long ago.

This page: *Interior showroom shots of EG Everton Glass tile displays (top left and top right) and wallpaper displays (left and above).*

The Venmore Group

The Name in Property

The Venmore Group is the largest local independent firm of chartered surveyors, estate agents, valuers, auctioneers, and property managers. It's a business that covers North Wales, Wirral, Southport as well as its Liverpool core. In 2014 they sold £250m worth of properties. The business is run by Paul Lea and Rob Farnham, the majority shareholders in Bradshaw Farnham & Lea, who bought Venmore in 2008.

The value of properties sold encompass the most expensive property sold on Merseyside and through the auction some of the lowest priced properties.

To find the roots of the Venmore Group you have to go back more than a century and a half.

The original firm of Thomas & Jones was founded in the 1850s and the founding partners were estate agents in the original sense of the words.

They managed rows of terraced houses collecting the rent, organising repairs, dealing with re-letting and acting on behalf of the owners.

Both founders were Welsh and they worked for the many Welsh builders who were then active in Liverpool. Mr Thomas left within four years but Mr Jones continued to expand the business. During the inter-war years he briefly took his son into the firm, but that association did not last.

In the 1930s the business was acquired by a Mr Russell who took a Mr Lloyd-Jones into partnership after the Second World War. They continued until the mid-1950s when Mr Russell retired and Mr Lloyd Jones died suddenly soon afterwards. For some time the business was run by Peter Jones, who started as an assistant in 1959, and office manager George Morgan on behalf of Lloyd-Jones' widow, and eventually this pair bought the firm.

Mike Earl joined in 1960 at a time when the firm was expanding, mainly by providing valuation and survey services to Building Societies.

Top: *The Group's new premises at Allerton, 8 – 10 Allerton Road, Liverpool, L18 1LN.* ***Left:*** *James Venmore, founder partner of W&J Venmore.*

The Partnership acquired several small property management businesses in the 1960s including that of Herbert Davies in Birkenhead which took the firm into a new area of business - design work.

Peter Jones was also involved with the formation of the Liver Housing Association in 1966 when a group of professionals came together to help provide quality rented housing. He was joined by, among others, Lawrence Jones of Thomas R Jones and Sons solicitors, Mr R Black of Page, Burne and Black accountants and local MP Richard Crawshaw.
By the end of its first 25 years the Association would be receiving annual income in rents of almost £6 million from hundreds of new homes.

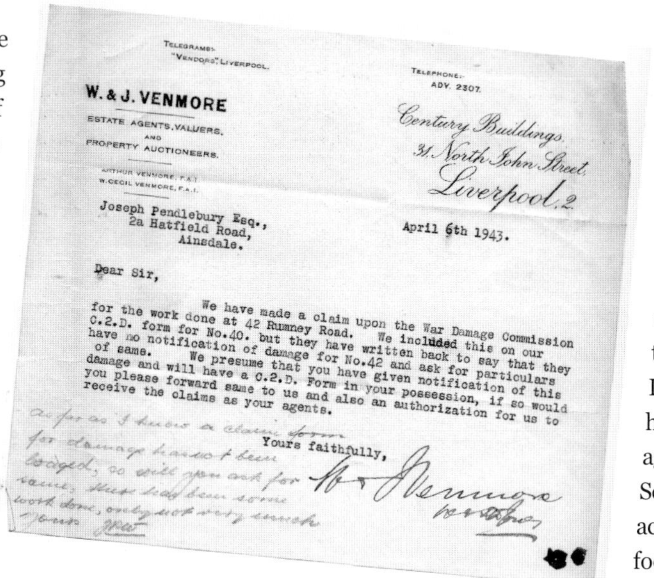

TELEGRAMS: "VENDORS" LIVERPOOL.

TELEPHONE: ADY. 2307.

W. & J. VENMORE

ESTATE AGENTS, VALUERS, AND PROPERTY AUCTIONEERS.

ARTHUR VENMORE, F.A.I.
W. CECIL VENMORE, F.A.I.

Century Buildings,
31, North John Street,
Liverpool, 2

Joseph Pendlebury Esq.,
2a Hatfield Road,
Ainsdale.

April 6th 1943.

Dear Sir,

We have made a claim upon the War Damage Commission for the work done at 42 Rumney Road. We included this on our C.2.D. form for No.40. but they have written back to say that they have no notification of damage for No.42 and ask for particulars of same. We presume that you have given notification of this damage and will have a C.2.D. Form in your possession, if so would you please forward same to us and also an authorization for us to receive the claims as your agents.

Yours faithfully,

as far as I know a claim form for damage has not been lodged, so will you ask for same, there has been some work done, only not very much

George Morgan retired in 1973; four years after Mike Earl had become a partner. In 1976 Thomas & Jones acquired the firm of Patterson & Thomas, from whom David Jones was to join the Partnership.

Patterson & Thomas was founded in 1849 and for much of its existence had occupied a Grade One listed building in Cook Street. Thomas & Jones were next door, and so a bridge was built between the two buildings. The merger meant that Thomas & Jones now included commercial property work as part of the practice and David Jones and David Inman dealt with this part of the business.

Meanwhile, the survey business had expanded and Derek Coates joined as a partner in the mid 1970s.

The firm's Drawing Office and Building Surveying side had grown from a tiny start following the earlier purchase of Herbert Davis, but that side of the business would split away from Thomas & Jones in the 1980s.

It was also in this decade that discussions with the firm of W&J Venmore led to the amalgamation of the two firms into Venmore, Thomas & Jones. W&J Venmore had taken its name from twin brothers William and James Venmore sons of the High Sheriff of Anglesey. In the late 19th Century they had established an estate agents business in Liverpool's Scotland Road. James would actually follow in his father's footsteps to become High Sheriff of Anglesey.

James Venmore's sons, Arthur and Cecil, would carry on the family business after the deaths of their father and uncle who, curiously, died within eight hours of each other in December 1920.

They were joined in 1936 by C Roger Morton. Arthur and Cecil died in 1961 and 1974 respectively and Roger, who had won a VC during the war, ran the partnership with the third generation of the Venmore family, Neville Venmore, until Neville's death in 1972. The street's surrounding Anfield include Venmore Street, named after the founders.

Above: *A letter dated April 1943 from W. & J. Venmore acting as agents for a claim upon the War Damage Commission.* ***Left and below:*** *War damaged houses in Carisbrook Road (left) and Berwyn Road.*

Miles Pickering then joined the firm which was going from strength to strength helped by Roger's deep local knowledge.

It was following Roger's retirement that, due to the size of the firm, Miles Pickering had to seek assistance, which resulted in the amalgamation with Thomas & Jones.

In Southport, the firm of Ball & Percival had been established in 1900 by Walter Knight Ball and a Mr Percival but their partnership split up early on leaving just Walter.

An advert in a local newspaper in 1900 refers to him having previously had 11 years' experience with a firm called Hindle & Son. The new business was established as a firm of auctioneers, valuers, estate and insurance agents, mortgage brokers and accountants with offices at St George's Place.

In 1905 the business relocated to the premises it still occupies in Lord Street.

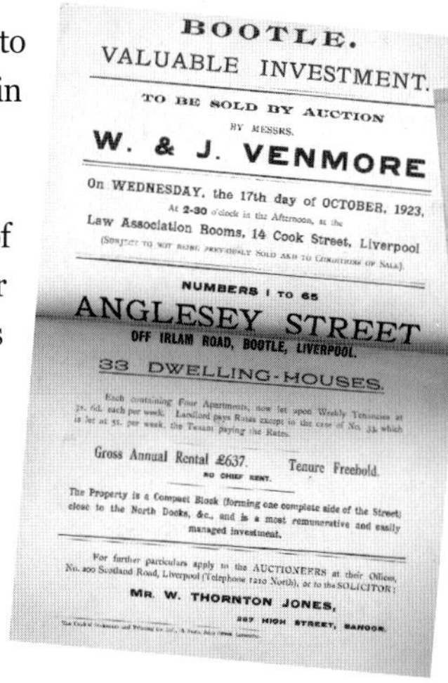
BOOTLE.
VALUABLE INVESTMENT.
TO BE SOLD BY AUCTION
BY MESSRS.
W. & J. VENMORE
On WEDNESDAY, the 17th day of OCTOBER, 1923,
At 2-30 o'clock in the Afternoon, at the
Law Association Rooms, 14 Cook Street, Liverpool
NUMBERS 1 TO 65
ANGLESEY STREET
OFF IRLAM ROAD, BOOTLE, LIVERPOOL.
33 DWELLING-HOUSES.
Gross Annual Rental £637. Tenure Freehold.
NO CHIEF RENT.
The Property is a Compact Block (forming one complete side of the Street) close to the North Docks, &c., and is a most remunerative and easily managed investment.
For further particulars apply to the AUCTIONEERS at their Offices, No. 200 Scotland Road, Liverpool (Telephone 1210 North), or to the SOLICITOR:
MR. W. THORNTON JONES,
287 HIGH STREET, BANGOR.

Raymond Knight Ball, one of Walter Ball's sons, took over the firm on his father's retirement in the 1930s, and in the 1940s the first non-family members became partners. Raymond Ball retired in 1964, a year after Bruce Jones joined the firm.

It continued to prosper as an independent partnership and in 1986 it became a limited company and was taken over by Hambro Countrywide Plc, the largest estate agency chain in the country.

Hambro's initial philosophy was to retain established trading names, and the business continued to trade as Ball & Percival. In

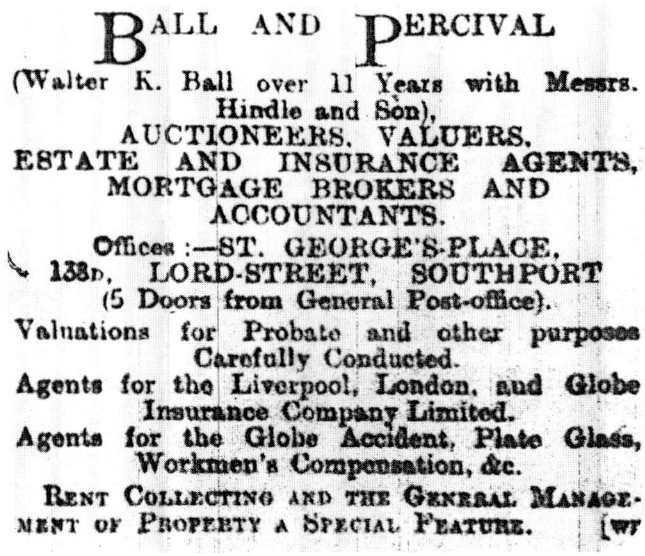
BALL AND PERCIVAL
(Walter K. Ball over 11 Years with Messrs. Hindle and Son),
AUCTIONEERS, VALUERS, ESTATE AND INSURANCE AGENTS, MORTGAGE BROKERS AND ACCOUNTANTS.
Offices :—ST. GEORGE'S-PLACE, 133D, LORD-STREET, SOUTHPORT
(5 Doors from General Post-office).
Valuations for Probate and other purposes Carefully Conducted.
Agents for the Liverpool, London, and Globe Insurance Company Limited.
Agents for the Globe Accident, Plate Glass, Workmen's Compensation, &c.
RENT COLLECTING AND THE GENERAL MANAGEMENT OF PROPERTY A SPECIAL FEATURE. [wr

1988 however, there was a name change, followed by a subsequent decline for the business.

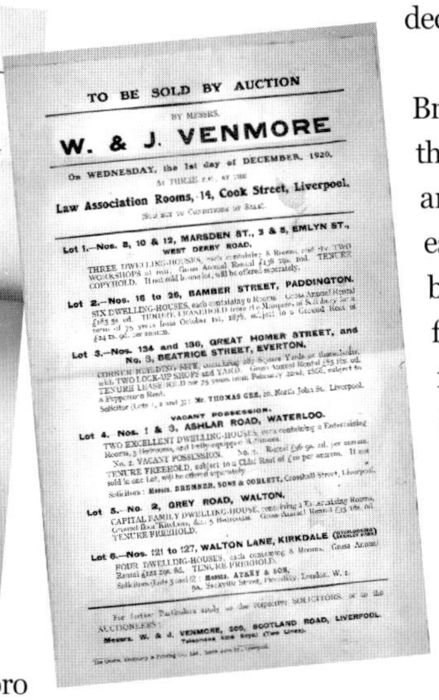
TO BE SOLD BY AUCTION
BY MESSRS.
W. & J. VENMORE
On WEDNESDAY, the 1st day of DECEMBER, 1920,
Law Association Rooms, 14, Cook Street, Liverpool.
Lot 1.—Nos. 8, 10 & 12, MARSDEN ST., 3 & 5, EMLYN ST., WEST DERBY ROAD.
Lot 2.—Nos. 16 to 26, BAMBER STREET, PADDINGTON.
Lot 3.—Nos. 134 and 136, GREAT HOMER STREET, and No. 3, BEATRICE STREET, EVERTON.
VACANT POSSESSION.
Lot 4. Nos. 1 & 3, ASHLAR ROAD, WATERLOO.
Lot 5.—No. 2, GREY ROAD, WALTON.
Lot 6.—Nos. 121 to 127, WALTON LANE, KIRKDALE
Messrs. W. & J. VENMORE, 200, SCOTLAND ROAD, LIVERPOOL.

Bruce Jones resigned his directorship on the change of name at the end of 1988 and with a business colleague he established a property consultancy. He bought back the professional side of the former Ball & Percival business in 1990, trading from 21 Hoghton Street in Southport. In 1991 he was concerned to see his former business in decline, and though still occupying its four-storey building it was only utilising the ground floor. A buy-back of what was left of the business was agreed later that year.

At the same time Ball & Percival, now led by Bruce Jones, merged with the even longer established practice of Venmore, Thomas & Jones in Liverpool.

Following further restructuring of the practice during 2005, which would eventually see the firm transfer in to a Limited Liability Partnership (LLP), it saw the retirement of some of the key drivers in the business and the promotion of a number of the firm's associates to Partner level.

Top right: *An advertisement for Ball and Percival, 1900.* ***Centre left:*** *Details for the auction of numbers 1 to 65 Anglesey Street, Bootle in 1923.* ***Centre right:*** *Lots for auction in the 1920s.* ***Left:*** *The firm's Lord Street, Southport, office.*

This change coincided with the beginning of the worst financial crisis in 100 years with the property market being caught in the eye of a perfect storm causing the business to retract and come close to going out of business.

Venmore was struggling having taken on a rapid expansion plan and didn't react quickly enough when the storm clouds of the demise of banks such as Northern Rock gathered.

As the business wavered and salaries hadn't been paid Bradshaw Farnham and Lea Ltd, a well-established Wirral business, bought the business and restructured it to fit the prevailing economic climate. They also relocated the business to a prominent Dale Street position announcing to all that Venmores is here in the City as its oldest property company.

Top left: *Venmore Auction Team Photo, Geoff Guest Director of Auctions (centre left) and the Auction team.* ***Above:*** *Sonia Mumford Roach, Area Director for Bradshaw Farnham & Lea* ***Below:*** *Paul Lea, Chairman, and Rob Farnham, Chief Executive.*

Rob Farnham and Paul Lea had an association with Venmore dating back to the late 1980s when they were frequent purchasers at the Venmore Auction. From this early business association and a trust formed on the rugby pitch wearing the colours of Hoylake, Bradshaw Farnham and Lea started. Having grown organically and through acquisition, they were in a strong position to keep the names of Venmore and Ball and Percival alive and begin the rebuilding and growth process.

Bradshaw Farnham & Lea are market leaders in most of the Wirral towns they operate in, specifically in the West Wirral where the business was founded.

The business has recovered and grown during the recession and is once again a strong player in the local property scene, moving with the changes in market to provide a service that encompasses; surveying, conveyancing and financial services as well as the core offering of sales, management and auction. The past twelve months has also seen growth in the commercial arm of the business and the business has adapted to the changes in the market that the internet has brought. The Auction business is headed by Geoff Guest, another Hoylake RFC stalwart and is regaining its position of strength and remains in the top ten auction houses in the UK.

Brookes Bell

A World of Marine Expertise

Based in Martins Building in Water Street, Liverpool, and in business for more than a century, the Brookes Bell Group operate from Liverpool, London, Glasgow, Shanghai, Hong Kong and Singapore.

Founded in 1903, Brookes Bell leads the market in professional expertise and experience across all the major maritime and scientific disciplines. All the full-time personnel work exclusively for the Group, enabling it to provide specialist advice in a wide range of inter-disciplinary areas.

Brookes Bell combines a wealth of practical experience with cutting-edge technology. This extraordinary skill set is the product of forensic investigation, tested to the highest level by providing expert evidence in courts and arbitrations worldwide, combined with innovative and advanced computational and analytical techniques used to promote safety at sea. The Group is active in research and development, ship design, innovative software to enhance marine safety, ship building advice and problem solving, marine scientific and technical consultancy, marine surveying, casualty investigation and product development.

The history of Brookes Bell can be traced back to a retired naval officer named Frederick H. Smith. He practised as a Marine Surveyor and Naval Architect from Fenwick Chambers in Liverpool. Frederick Smith had seen active service as an engineer in the Royal Navy and had been on one of the gunboats which had supported the British Army in its belated and unsuccessful expedition up the River Nile to relieve General Gordon at Khartoum in 1885. Smith's office was next door to that of James R. Ellerman, agent for the City Line of steamships. Just after the First World War Frederick Smith formed a partnership, 'Smith, Brookes and Sumner', with Percy W. Brookes and Thomas Sumner, with offices in James Street.

In the 1920s Frederick Smith retired, although he went on to live to over 100.

Thomas Sumner was less fortunate. In the 1930s he was one of a large number of Liverpool surveyors who would begin their day's work on board ship in the docks at daybreak. Following a hard morning's surveying they would convene at lunchtime in a hostelry before a more leisurely afternoon writing up reports.

Left: *A post-war view of the Martins Building, home to Brookes Bell, Liverpool.* ***Above:*** *The Mersey Ferry docking at the floating landing stage, Liverpool Docks, 1910.*

These were the days when Liverpool, along with all industrial cities in the country, suffered from dense fogs. One fatal day Sumner left his lunchtime retreat and stepped out into such a fog to visit the Harland and Wolff shipyard along the Dock Road. Sumner availed himself of the time-honoured tradition of following the tram lines through the fog, certain in the knowledge that the trams ceased to run when the fog descended. Unfortunately, on this occasion, one tram was making its way back to the depot when it encountered Sumner striding along with his umbrella ferrule acting as a guide in the tram line. And that was the end of Thomas Sumner!

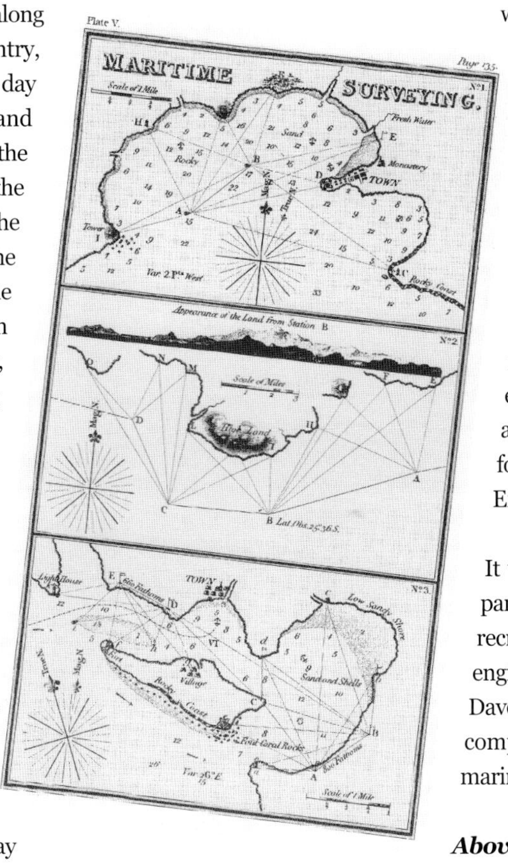

Percy Brookes was subsequently joined by Robert Bell, known as 'Bobby'. Together they formed Brookes, Bell & Company. They practiced as Naval Architects, Consulting Engineers, Marine and Cargo Surveyors from the Mersey Railway Buildings on James Street. The company remained in those offices until after the Second World War, moving to Tower Building, Water Street, in 1950.

Percy Brookes too had met a dramatic end. In the Blitz of Liverpool during the war, Brookes' home and his office were both hit by bombs. It was assumed he was in one, or the other, but his body was never found.

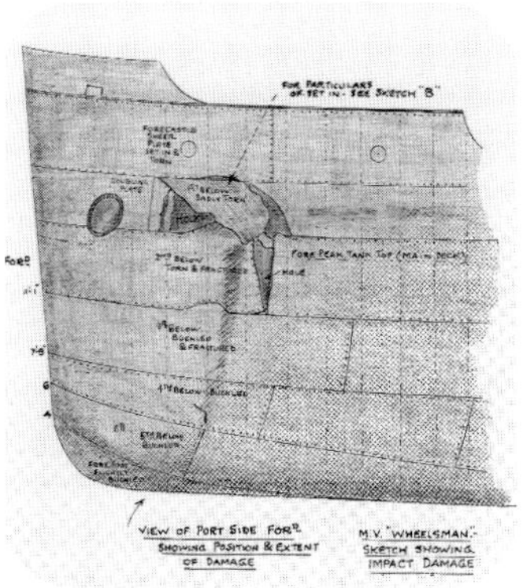

Following Brookes' untimely end the firm passed into the hands of George Crellin, a sole practitioner. Crellin claimed to have a Square-Rigger Master's licence, although it was widely believed within the Liverpool surveying fraternity that his experience on sailing ships had only been as a Bosun. Crellin was a familiar figure in the Liverpool docks, always sporting a walking cane and bowler hat, and accompanied by his terrier dog.

The firm was acquired from George Crellin by James 'Jim' Gornall in 1959. He was soon to be joined by Peter Smith. Both had been working ashore for stevedoring companies after serving at sea with Cunard.

In those days Brookes Bell was dedicated to providing essential services to the shipping industry in the Port of Liverpool. The firm grew steadily under the leadership of Gornall and Smith, later joined by John Knott, and it was these three individuals who developed the firm's reputation for knowledge, integrity and efficiency which was so attractive to clients, although their operations remained largely focused in Liverpool and the North-West of England.

It was not until the mid-1970s that the three partners were sufficiently confident to start recruiting the next generation of deck and engineer officers, headed by John Maxwell and Dave Spence. It was they who now led the company's expansion into the international marine survey business.

Above: *Examples of early Marine Surveying from the Treatise on Practical Navigation.* ***Below left:*** *In the absence of photographic supplies during, and immediately after the war years, detailed drawings such as these were made to illustrate damages sustained.* ***Below:*** *The Europa, a large Dutch ship which was bombed and sunk twice while in dock.*

The need to offer a more convenient service to the clients was recognised by the decision to open an office in London. In June 1985 Brookes Bell became one of the first tenants of the London Dockland Development Zone, at the historic Cannon Workshops.

In 1988 Jim Gornall and Peter Smith retired, having firmly established Brookes Bell as Consultants and Marine Experts known throughout the shipping and marine insurance industry.

In 1993, the London office of the firm moved to modern premises at Harbour Exchange Building.

A major turning point came in 1998 when Brookes Bell merged with Jarrett Kirman & Partners. Jarrett Kirman could be traced back to the 1960s when John Kirman became a partner of the inimitable Dr. Reg Milton before setting up Jarrett Kirman and Willems partnership in 1985. Working from offices in Harpenden and Rotterdam, they built up a reputation for excellence as consulting scientists. The integration of the scientists with Brookes Bell's Master Mariners, Naval Architects and Marine Engineers proved an immediate and ongoing success.

The need to house additional staff and offer an increased range of professional disciplines to clients led to a move to Butlers Wharf in London and the opening of an office in Sidcup in 2001. By 2010, the Partners had agreed on a strategy of growth, diversification and expansion into Asia. By the end of that year Brookes Bell had commenced operations in Shanghai.

In 2011 Brookes Bell acquired Bunker Claims International to supplement its marine fuel expertise, and Safety at Sea also joined Brookes Bell. Safety at Sea, now a wholly owned company, is a leading expert in the stability, design and safe operation of ships and advanced marine vehicles ranging from concept design through to delivering innovative products and services. Later that year Robert Vart rejoined Brookes Bell to form Brookes Bell Hong Kong.

In 2012, Brookes Bell Research and Development began operation. The Group also opened in Singapore with a core team of loss adjusters to work alongside traditional marine consultants to establish the Brookes Bell Group in the offshore energy market.

Most recently, in 2014, Brookes Bell Metallurgical Services opened a new facility for metallurgical inspection and storage of samples and machinery parts for marine and offshore investigations.

This page: *A selection from Brookes Bell past case history. Top left shows the extensive damage to the bows of the VLCC 'Skyron'. Left is the raising of the hull of the Indonesian vessel 'Andhika Samyra' after an explosion and fire off Jakarta and above shows a container crane struck by a vessel berthing at Port Kelang, Indonesia.*

It's no wonder that whenever help is required - and quickly - the marine and energy industries turn to Brookes Bell.

In all disciplines, the Group can and does act as expert witnesses in arbitrations and courts worldwide. The team now includes master mariners, marine engineers, naval architects, scientists, metallurgists, loss adjusters and fire investigators and continues to expand both in numbers and services offered to clients.

Brookes Bell leads the market in marine, scientific and technical consultancy and casualty investigation. The Group's investigations include ship operations and cargoes, whether operating as emergency response, attending at the site of a problem, or simply providing document-based opinions.

Cargo scientists are complemented from the UK offices by fuel chemists dealing mainly with fuel and liquid chemical claims, metallurgists who focus on failure investigation and fire investigators with many years' experience.

Safety at Sea Ltd, part of the Group, brings together specialists in seakeeping, manoeuvring, stability, hydrodynamics, fire protection, evacuation as well as safety engineering and risk analysis. Safety at Sea has also advised on and carried out studies for clients in various aspects of port design and operations.

The company possesses advanced engineering analysis capabilities utilising both commercially available and unique, in-house software tools under continuous development. Brookes Bell also provides training courses such as 'At the Sharp End' a practical short course covering merchant ships and their operations.

The Brookes Bell story is indeed a remarkable one. From its founding in 1903 by Frederick Smith it has grown over the course of more than a century to become world-renowned – but nowhere is that reputation more deserved than in its home port of Liverpool.

Top left, left, bottom left and above: *Some of Brookes Bell's relatively recent technical and forensic assignments.* ***Below:*** *A montage of Brookes Bell experts at work.*

GETRAG FORD Transmissions

Better Together

The names 'Ford' and 'Halewood' are inextricably linked. In recent years, however, the Halewood Transmission Plant has been operated under the rather less familiar name of GETRAG FORD Transmissions.

For the younger generation the Halewood Transmission Plant had been part of the Liverpool scene forever: but when the Beatles first began to play Halewood was still an area of wild roses and strawberry fields. 1964 was a year to remember. For Liverpool a new era was just opening: the arrival of the Ford Motor Company at Halewood.

Two red roses picked on Midsummer's day were once the annual rent for the land on which the Halewood factory stands. The blooms were handed over by the Ireland family to the area's wealthiest landlord, Lord Derby. Lord Derby may well have chosen the peppercorn rent instead of money because he was tired of the endless bickering over land along the banks of the Mersey. Or maybe he was just a keen rose-lover who couldn't bother to cut the blooms for table decorations himself.

Ford planned to focus its latest expansion programme in Dagenham. The Government. however, was insistent that expansion should be channelled into distressed areas of Britain. And there were 27,000 unemployed in Merseyside. The choice of Halewood for an £8.5 million investment was made in September 1962.

Halewood was selected for several reasons:

First, the 346-acre site allowed plenty of room for future developments. The site was also well supplied with gas, electricity, fuel oil and water. The estate also enjoyed good communications: on the North side was the Liverpool to London railway line providing Ford with a high speed 'conveyor line' between Halewood and Dagenham. Trains would travel between

Halewood and Dagenham every day bringing engines, rear axles and forgings and castings, and carrying away gearboxes, stampings and trim. Thirty-five trains would leave Halewood and Garston every week for distribution points throughout the country.

***Top:** An aerial view of Halewood Transmission Plant site, part of Ford's industrial estate which covers 346 acres to the south of Liverpool. **Left:** Ray Knott operating a Talyrond measuring machine. **Above:** Margaret Thatcher, then leader of the Opposition was a VIP visitor to the plant in 1978.*

On the South side were good roads. The Speke Boulevard, built as a joint venture between Liverpool Corporation, Lancashire County Council and Ford, was built to expressway standards. The plant would also be close to the planned M62. The good roads provided an excellent and rapid route for suppliers, whilst also enabling employees to clear the plant in less than ten minutes at shift change. Good docking facilities at Garston and Liverpool were also a significant advantage. Liverpool Airport, less than a mile way, provided an ideal pick-up point for air-freighted supplies and executive travellers. The sheer distance from Dagenham, however, created extra transport costs, whilst also facing the company with recruiting in an area which had no previous experience of the industry.

Ford established the largest and most comprehensive training programme ever undertaken by British industry - £2 million was spent on training before a single car was built. Ford established a mock production line in an aircraft hanger at Liverpool Airport, where the first recruits were trained whilst the plant itself was being constructed. The first 30 Merseyside employees were recruited on 1st January 1962. Altogether 8,000 workers were given training. There was also a management development programme. The new management team at Halewood –one of the youngest in the country – was sent on training courses tailored to suit individual's particular needs. Another important part of the training programme was the trainee foreman scheme in which potential supervisors were given six months training on such subjects as work-study, industrial relations and communications.

Three hundred key personnel from Dagenham (and later from Doncaster) were brought up to Halewood to train new recruits. The same pattern was repeated when the transmission plant was built at Heywood when a special training centre was established at Kirkby.

The original factory was completed in 1964, constructed for the production and assembly of light, medium and heavy car transmissions. The factory was adjacent to Ford's new Stamping and Assembly Plants (then under construction, and which would complete the first car made on Merseyside on 8th March 1963).

Halewood's Transmission Plant would be the most technically advanced factory of its kind in the world, making gearboxes for Ford's entire range. No craftsman could hope to match the precision of the 2,000 production machines, far less the array of complex and costly equipment installed to ensure consistently high quality.

Construction took just 16 months. It was one of the fastest plant building operations ever to take place in Britain, as well as being one of the first in which the 'critical path' method of planning – a revolutionary step – would be employed.

Top left: *Presentation of Foremanship Certificates, April 1979.* ***Left:*** *Tommy Smith (the then plant manager) and Derek Smith present Henry Ford II with a memento of Merseyside on his visit to Halewood Transmission Plant.* ***Below:*** *Civil dignitaries from Liverpool, Knowsley and Halewood were guests when the production milestones of 10,000,000 gearboxes was reached.*

A special operations room was set up on site to administer the construction, with a computer calculating the most effective and direct ways of building. Deadlines for completion of the various phases of construction together with manpower requirements and schedules for the supply of materials were also calculated. Alternative courses of action were planned for in case of any hold-up in the critical path due to unforeseen factors.

Though many machines were new, hundreds more were transferred from Dagenham. As a Dagenham machine was shut down on a Friday night it was dismantled, shipped to Halewood and reassembled for use on Monday. The total plant personnel would be 3,000, with a projected daily output of more than one gearbox for every employee. A seven-bay extension was added to the east side of the building in 1966 to accommodate the production of chassis and steering components, increasing the total area of the plant to over a million square feet. A further two-bays were built in 1978/79 on the plant's west side for the launch of the new front-wheel drive Escort transaxle bringing the total area to 1.2 million square feet.

Liverpool celebrated in 1978 when the three-millionth Ford vehicle, an Escort, rolled off the production line.

On the plant's 25th birthday, its Silver Jubilee, in 1989, a head count revealed no fewer than 425 employees had each been with the firm since the day it had opened.

By the turn of the millennium Halewood had become a joint Ford-Jaguar site comprising a vehicle Assembly Plant and a Manual Transmissions Operations Plant. Investment was being planned to re-equip for prestigious Jaguar production with the whole site intended to employ 4,000 people, 3,000 aligned to the Jaguar Plant. By then the Manual Transmission Operations Plant was employing around 1,000 people.

Ford described its 'prime asset' as 'the depth of automotive technical skill inherent within the local workforce...one of the most highly skilled and technically competent work forces in Europe'.

***Top left:** Plant manager Bob Taylor receives the award for 2005 Best Engineering Plant.* ***Left:** Celebrations as the 15 millionth transaxle is produced.* ***Above:** HRH Prince Andrew visits the plant in 2005 to celebrate the many awards and achievements received by the company.*

Since 2001 the plant has been operated by GETRAG FORD Transmissions.

GETRAG FORD Transmissions was founded as a joint venture between the transmission specialist GETRAG, based in Untergruppen-bach (Baden-Württemberg), and the Ford Motor Company. The purpose of the joint venture was to combine the strengths of both partners in the field of manual and automated manual transmissions. The parent companies each contributed skilled personnel, a state-of-the-art product development centre, production plants, know-how and capital.

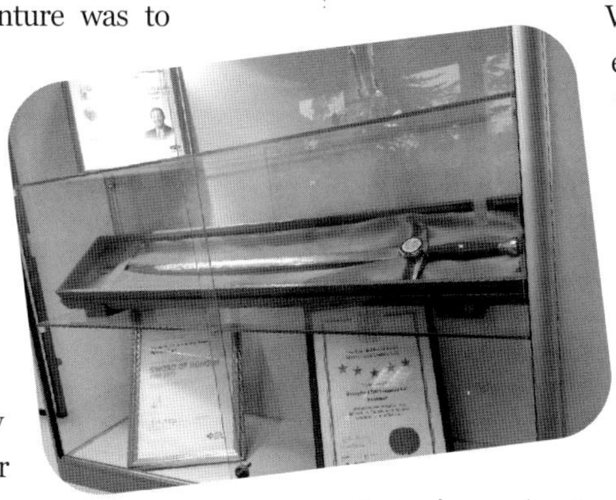

The company has since won several new customers, including Mazda, MG Rover and Volvo.

Services include not only developing and producing transmissions, but also developing and delivering components and shifter controls, integrating transmission systems into vehicles and providing the engineering services.

Halewood welcomed the first GFT contracted employees into the workforce in 2007. Today, the transmissions plant employs around 800 staff.

In October 2010 Getrag Ford Transmissions launched a brand new six-speed manual transmission, following an investment of some 100 million Euros.

This state-of-the-art transmission was developed for small and compact front wheel drive vehicles for Ford, Volvo and Mazda. Production volumes are expected to reach 500,000 units annually. "This is a very important product for our plant and came at the right time", says Alan Seeley, the Halewood Plant HR Manager. "This increased demand will safeguard our future and is also good news for the Northwest of England and Merseyside as a whole". The new Giorgio 6 Speed Rear Wheel Drive Transmission will be produced in Halewood starting at the end of 2015, increasing to maximum volume in 2018. That good news, coming at the end of the Plant's 50 Year celebrations in 2014, included an investment of 30 million Euros.

Top: *A recent view inside the GFT plant.* ***Centre:*** *In 2011 Halewood were awarded the British Safety Council (BSC) 5 Star Award for Safety and in 2012 the BSC Sword of Honour.* ***Left:*** *The B6 Gear Cutting Team received an award for their achievement of 1,000 days without an accident.* ***Above:*** *GFT welcome the public to a charity event at the plant.*

Nugent Care

Helping Others Since 1881

Nugent Care is one of the oldest and largest charities in Liverpool. The organisation offers a wide range of support to vulnerable and disadvantaged adults and children throughout Merseyside and parts of the North West of England.

Father James Nugent was born in 1822. Lord Canning – who had been a local MP until a few years earlier – was Foreign Secretary. Canning described Liverpool as the most corrupt constituency in the realm: "they would drink your drink, and eat your food, and run off with your wives" he said, "and they'll vote for someone else". Voting criteria of the time were less than inclusive. Only men were entitled to vote, and then only if they had an acre of land, or £40.

Lime Street was beyond the town's boundaries, and a trip to Woolton would have taken half a day by coach. Liverpool was essentially a village – records show that the big story that year was John Dennison's church windows. Dennison thought that the church of St Peter's needed new windows, so he paid £189 for them personally. Each year, Dennison claimed reimbursement from the parish, and each year he was rejected – despite his friends putting in an annual 'Dennison wants his money back' motion.

James Nugent was born the eldest child of John and Mary, he was baptised at St Nicholas', Copperas Hill – the church which Roman Catholics in the city then referred to as their Cathedral Church. Education was limited, and James' family didn't have enough money to send him to public school. Instead he went to the James Picton Academy. In 1838, he attended St Cuthbert's College in Ushaw – which was one of the great Catholic foundations of the day – and after that, the English College in Rome. Nugent was ordained at St Nicholas' on Copperas Hill in 1846, at which time Liverpool was in the throes of a severe population crisis: an incredible influx of people swelled the population; many travelling from Ireland, many of them disaffected, and many using Liverpool's port as a gateway to the New World. An increased population meant that many people in Liverpool lived in appalling squalor.

It was during the famine of 1846 that Nugent began to minister Liverpool's poor. New ministers and priests were also needed to replace those who had died of fever.

Famine was followed by a cholera epidemic in 1849, and 5,244 people in Liverpool died within the first few months of the outbreak. Father Nugent served at the heart of this, working amongst the people and campaigning for Catholic schools, better health provision and social services.

Top left: *Portrait of Father James Nugent (1822-1905).* ***Left:*** *A Sketch of Hunter Street - the birthplace of Father Nugent.* ***Above:*** *A statue of Father Nugent in St John's Gardens which was unveiled in 1906.* ***Below:*** *The Clarence Reformatory School Ship for Boys, docked in the River Mersey.*

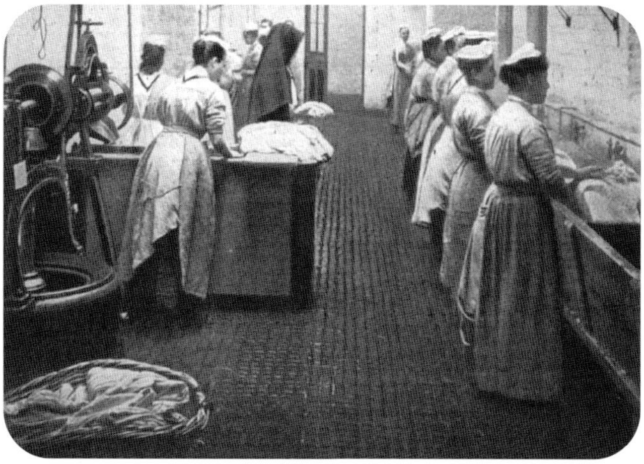

On 16th April, 1881, Father Nugent and his supporters founded the Liverpool Catholic Children's Protection Society, which after several name changes including; the Catholic Children's Society, Liverpool Catholic Social Services and the Nugent Care Society, became simply known as Nugent Care in 2005.

By the time of Father Nugent's death in 1905, he had given homes, hope and valuable skills to thousands of people. His dedication, courage and pioneering work laid the foundations for the support that Nugent Care offers to this very day.

Today, Nugent Care still carries on the work of Father Nugent with a wide range of services providing a highly individualised and tailored approach to all of its service users. Staff work with children, adults and community groups through residential care homes, schools and community projects throughout the North West, ensuring people's rights, independence, interdependence, choice and inclusion are integrated into everything they do.

One of the most recent developments is the Courtyard Café and Training Centre. The Courtyard is a healthy eating café based in Knowsley targeted to local businesses and the wider community. The aim of the café is to provide opportunity for adults with learning disabilities or people who are not in employment, education or training to gain industry standard qualifications for employability purpose. As a social care provider, Nugent Care works at the heart of some of the most vulnerable and disadvantaged communities. It strives not only to provide the best possible service to individuals and their families in these areas, but to generate interest, awareness and an understanding of the issues they face and the impact of this on the wider community.

Top left: *At work in the laundry room of the refuge shelter for women in Paul Street.* ***Left:*** *Nugent Care's Court Missionary visiting a family in Bevington Bush in the 1960s.* ***Above:*** *Phil Thompson (second right), Nugent Care's Patron, taking part in a cook off event at the Courtayrd Café and Training Centre.* ***Bottom left:*** *Lime House Lowton - a residential care home for older people living with dementia.* ***Bottom centre:*** *Clarence High School, Formby, which provides thirty eight week and fifty two week residential care and day placements for boys and girls who have a statement of Special Educational Needs (SEN).* ***Bottom right:*** *Clumber Care Children's Home - a residential and therapeutic care home for children and young people with emotional and behavioural difficulties and learning disabilities. There is a mother and baby assessment unit on site supporting the needs of the young mothers and their babies. All services and projects run by Nugent Care can be seen on their website: www.nugentcare.org*

FRANK ROGERS BUILDING CONTRACTOR LTD

BUILDING ON THEIR EXPERIENCE

Frank Rogers Building Contractor Ltd, based at The Stables, Larkhill Lane, Liverpool, was established in 1972. The family-owned company enjoys an increasing annual turnover of £10 million. Predominantly working throughout the North West, the firm has progressively developed the resources, expertise and experience to successfully undertake a wide range of construction projects.

Frank Rogers was a Joiner by trade, and served his apprenticeship in the mid-1960s with Joseph Broster and Sons Ltd. In the early 1970s he set up his own fencing and general repairs company. Frank's big break came in 1974 when he began working with Merseyside Improved Housing (now Riverside). In 1975 he won his first major contract carrying out extensive housing improvements on twelve properties in Liverpool 5 – Norgate Street, next to Sleepers Hill. Frank Rogers soon secured more contracts, carrying out works for a number of Registered Social Landlords across the North of Merseyside. Frank initially started working from home, before moving to a shop unit on Oakfield Road, Anfield. Frank stayed there until he refurbished and moved into an old Stables in Clubmoor, where the business still operates from today.

Frank's methods and approach to work was considered innovative – his first focus was improving properties in need of refurbishment and repair. He then went on to look at new builds and then expanded into commercial properties.

Top left: *Frank Rogers' premises, The Stables, in Larkhill Lane.* ***Left:*** *Founder, Frank Rogers.* ***Above:*** *Where it all began - Frank and his Transit van outside on one of their first refurbishment jobs in Norgate Street in the 1970s.* ***Below:*** *Frank Rogers' former premises in Oakfield Road.*

Frank's son, Dean, joined the business in 2002, having previously worked as a Procurement Manager for a Telecoms Company. Dean worked closely with his father on an operational level, and took over as Managing Director following his father's death in 2009. Frank's wife, Cath, and Daughter, Lisa, are also Directors and both work in the family business.

Employing the majority of its 70-plus skilled workforce directly, Frank Rogers' typical contracts range from large-scale bathroom, kitchen and window replacement programmes to void refurbishments, fire risk works, and disabled adaptations.

Today, Frank Rogers offers a complete housing refurbishment or upgrade solution from ground up, internal and external, up to roof area. Customers are able to task Frank Rogers with multiple elements of a refurbishment and know that all works are being managed by a single company.

New build and refurbishment of commercial properties, public and heritage building also form part of the Frank Rogers business. Dean Rogers says: "Through our long term, repeat business associations with many of Merseyside's social landlords, we have been able to hone a business model that works incredibly well. By using local skilled labour, good tenant liaison with solid project management and back end admin support, we are able to deliver a project of almost any scale and size to a successful outcome. Our flexible approach means that we're able to look at the smallest of contracts to multi-million pound long term frameworks and deliver each one to the same standard using the same approach. I believe that it's this attitude that has allowed us to grow to the stage at which we're at today, using a strategic and cautious approach."

The company takes pride in employing highly skilled local people who have helped develop the reputation that the firm enjoys today. That performance is also supported by the long-term established relationships with reputable sub-contractors and suppliers.

A lot of the firm's work is maintenance for housing associations. Other work is carried out for large private landlords, local authorities, hospitals and schools.

After four decades of trading, the company offers a full range of services including new build, refurbishment and responsive works, as well as private developments through its sister company FR Developments. Keen to embrace change and work with new technologies, products, materials and ways of working, the firm blends traditional approach with modern and employs the most suitable elements from each for every project.

Most recently the company has been developing its Greener Solutions Division, working with homeowners, landlords and private businesses, installing green measures at thousands of properties across the North West.

For the future Frank Rogers plans to consolidate business and expand within the North West, offering more of the same services but on a wider scale.

Above left: *Dean Rogers, Manging Director, with fellow Directors and Mum and Sister, Cath Rogers and Lisa Blake.* ***Above right:*** *A Frank Rogers van.* ***Left and below:*** *Frank Rogers carried out a £1 million restoration of this dilapidated Grade II listed building (Elm Terrace) utilising a range of modern day and traditional technologies for Riverside Housing Association.*

Tilney Bestinvest

Sharing Prosperity

The name Tilney is deeply entwined with that of Liverpool. With offices in the Royal Liver Building, Tilney Bestinvest is a leading investment and financial planning firm that builds on a heritage of more than 150 years. The firm now looks after more than £9 billion on clients' behalf.

In 1836 Thomas Tinley and his second son, George, set up a firm for the purpose of dealing in stocks and shares, with offices at 7, Water Street. Thomas' third son, Robert, joined the firm in the 1840s. After their father's death in 1847 the two brothers continued to run the business until a quarrel led to their liquidation of the firm and the formation of R J Tilney & Co. When Robert Tilney died the business was carried on by executors until his son, Robert Henry, came of age.

In 1895, R J Tilney & Co took on Mr John Brocklebank at a salary of £70 a year. He became a partner in 1910 and later co-head of the firm with Col. Robert Henry Tilney.

During the First World War all three of Lieutenant Colonel Tilney's sons followed a military career. John Brocklebank, the remaining partner held the fort. However, disaster struck with the death in March 1918 of Major Leonard Arthur Tilney.

Above: *George A. Tilney (left) and Robert. J. Tilney.* ***Left:*** *Colonel Robert Henry Tilney.* ***Below:*** *The Liverpool Stock Market in the mid-19th century.* ***Right:*** *Major Leonard Arthur Tilney in his Royal Air Corps uniform shortly before he was killed in action in March 1918, aged just 22.*

Yet, as John Brocklebank later wrote, "The financial history of the war period worked out miraculously - all outstanding contracts completed, enormous loans paid off..."

The 1920s began brightly with the 'cotton boom'.

John Tilney joined the firm in 1928. Looking back Sir John remembered the old office in Castle Street with its tall desks at which the clerks stood to write up the ledgers, and the distress caused by the cotton crash of the 1930s.

At the outbreak of the Second World War R J Tilney had 17 male members of staff. Eleven joined the forces: three never returned.

John Tilney became MP for Wavertree in 1950, remaining so until 1974. Much of the day-to-day work in the fifties was covered by John Patrick Bingham. The easiest way to grow was through merger, the first of these being with Messrs Parr & Rae in 1958 to form Tilney, Parr & Rae. Sefton House became its new home.

The Northern Stock Exchange was formed in 1965. This led to new regulations about the minimum size of member firms. Tilney, Parr & Rae consequently acquired G H Chamberlain and Sing White. The combined Group, was known as Tilney, Sing, Parr & Rae. Over the next decade, however, personal investment declined because of the taxation policies of successive governments. The economic boom of the early 1970s was followed by rapidly rising inflation, penal taxation, higher interest rates and a banking crisis.Worse followed in 1974-5, partly caused by industrial unrest and partly by the rise in oil prices after the Arab-Israeli War. These led to a sharp fall in share prices. Staff numbers fell from 158 to just 64.

When the markets improved Tilney prospered, extending its business into the new areas of building, brewing and electronics, whilst the long-established dealing in shipping was extended.

Since regional stock exchanges had by now disbanded, a merger with Charles W Jones & Co made Tilney large enough to deal directly with the London Stock Exchange. In May 1986 Tilney was taken over by the Charterhouse Group. The Liverpool Head Office moved from Sefton House to the Royal Liver Building in 1988.

By 1993 a management buy-out of the private client division was effected with the name reverting to Tilney & Co. The name of the company changed to Tilney Investment Management in 1998. That same year Tilney linked itself to Forstmann-Leff. Tilney was acquired by Refco Group Holdings Ltd in 2000.

Five years later Tilney was reacquired by its management before being acquired by Deutsche Bank Group in 2006 as part of its Global Private Wealth Management Business and most recently, in 2014, Tilney amalgamated with Bestinvest to form 'Tilney Bestinvest'.

Headquartered in Mayfair, London, Tilney Bestinvest today employs almost 400 staff across a network of UK offices, combining award-winning research and expertise to provide a personalised service to clients whatever their investment needs.

Top left: *John Brocklebank.* ***Left and top right:*** *The Liverpool Stock Exchange in the 1950s.* ***Above:*** *One of the clock towers of the Royal Liver Building, an iconic symbol of Liverpool since 1911.*

ACKNOWLEDGMENTS

The publishers would like to sincerely thank the following individuals and organisations for their help and contribution to this publication.

Mirrorpix

dusashenka's photostream - www.flickr.com/photos/oldcinemaphotos/